CW00685786

ENGLISH RACING STABLES

English Racing Stables

ANDREW SIM

PHOTOGRAPHY BY
ANDREW SIM AND WILLIAM SHAW

DIAL
PRESS

TO THE MEMORY OF
VERA SPILLER

Acknowledgements:

I am indebted to all the trainers, past and present, who gave their time to help me with the research for this book. Without their help and enthusiasm for the project, a book on this scale would have been impossible. A posthumous word of thanks also to Lady Murless and Jeremy Tree, who both sadly died during the production of the book. They were both extremely helpful to me in my research and I would like to extend my sympathy to their respective families.

A special word of thanks must go to Elizabeth Carcasson, whose kind words, expert advice and practical help have been invaluable and inspirational. Thanks also to Marten Julian, Alastair Down and William Shaw for their professional assistance. None of this, of course, would have been possible without the help of a supportive family.

The publishers and I would like to thank the following agencies and individuals who supplied the photographs for the pages noted: Gerry Cranham (p34), Alec Russell (pp90, 122), A&B Photography (pp138 lower, 139 both), Dave Phillips (pp161–4).

Page1; *On the all weather gallop at Seven Barrows.*
Page3; *On the way to a day's work, Middleham.*

First published 1993
ISBN 0 7110 2158 9

Published by Dial Press.
Dial Press is an imprint of Ian Allan Publishing, Addlestone, Surrey.

Printed in Great Britain by
Ian Allan Printing Ltd,
Coombelands House, Addlestone, Surrey KT15 1HY.

Contents

Above: Warren Place, Newmarket soon after construction in 1928. (photograph courtesy Betty Dorney née Darling)

Below: Victorian Newmarket. Coming back home along a traffic-free High Street. (Racing Illustrated)

English Racing Stables

Introduction

Manton; Kinnersley; Kingsclere; Beckhampton; Greystoke. The names will be a familiar litany to any afficionado of the racing pages and yet, how many people actually know what these legendary places look like? Students of the form book will profess to know to the pound how a horse can be expected to perform on a given day but will know little or nothing about the character of the place where it is trained.

This is a book inspired by curiosity. As a racing obsessed schoolboy, checking the results in the newspaper to see how many winners Lester had managed the previous day, my eye was always drawn to the trainer's name, accompanied by locations that seemed, to me, mysterious and evocative: Maj.W.R.Hern, West Ilsley; J.Tree, Beckhampton; G.Todd, Manton. Talk of valley gallops on the downs, secret Derby trials and the like, bandied about on television and in newspapers, intensified my desire to know more.

Such curiosity is, of course, nothing new. In the days before the sporting press satisfied the racing public's craving for firsthand information about the well-being of a trainer's horses, itinerant bands of men made a tenuous living, creeping around the hedgerows on the fringes of racing estates in the hope of witnessing secret trials. In the not-so romantic days of Victorian gambling confederacies, secrecy was at such a premium that stable lads were locked in their dormitories at night, touts were shouted at, ridden over, beaten and, on one occasion at Kingsclere during the days of the great John Porter, simply locked in the labourer's hut they had been lurking in until the morning's exercise was over.

Mixed traffic hazards on the road to the Low Moor, Middleham.

At another level, much as trainers have always disliked the unwelcome intrusion of the touts, they have traditionally welcomed the opportunity to advertise the virtues of their training establishments. As soon as it became practicable, late nineteenth century photographers overcame all manner of technical difficulties to depict trainers and their strings in their pastoral context. The few surviving volumes of magazines like *Racing Illustrated* provide a fascinating glimpse of the landscape of British racing at the end of the nineteenth century. It was not simply the physical geography of the landscape or the horses, the names of which have mostly faded into obscurity, which fascinated *Racing Illustrated's* public

Brecongill today.

but the stables themselves, the trainer's house and gardens. Even the ubiquitous, motley collections of stable dogs (a tradition that continues to this day) were considered worthy of attention.

Many of the yards visited by those intrepid pioneers have disappeared altogether from the racing map. The oldest and arguably the most distinguished racing stable in the country, Palace House in Newmarket, is a boarded up, fire-damaged wreck. Others have mutated into different forms, becoming studs or livery yards, but such is the continuity of British racing, that a large number of the yards featured in *Racing Illustrated* in the 1890s continue to participate in 'the great triviality'. Some like Manton, have been radically altered and expanded, but others, such as Park House, Kingsclere, the home of the great John Porter, are virtually unchanged in a century. It is not just the great powerhouses of racing, either, that have remained intact. Apart from the removal of a superficial covering of ivy, John Osborne's Brecongill yard in Middleham is safe in Sally Hall's capable hands and Cree Lodge in Ayr is much the same as it was on the day it was opened by its first trainer, John McGuigan, in 1908.

There is, sadly, no equivalent of *Racing Illustrated* today. Touting may have become instutionalised in the form of guardedly polite workwatchers' reports from Newmarket Heath but, away from the business of tipping, remarkably little background material is transmitted to the general public about life in the average racing stable. There are numerous features in the *Sporting Life* and the *Racing Post* about trainers, but most concentrate on discussions of form and statistics rather than buildings, landscape and tradition. Despite the spread of ownership and the growth of racing clubs, training in Britain today is, by its very nature, as private as ever. The huge popularity of stable open days, when members of the public pay an entrance fee to take a peek behind the stable door, is proof of the level of public interest in this peculiarly enclosed world.

Although there are certain unalterable features in the diurnal ritual of a racing stable: the three lots, evening stables, etc, training in Britain is also extraordinarily varied. Unlike most other racing countries, where the sport is centralised, and trainers cluster together in anonymous stabling at their appointed place of work, training in Britain has always been widespread and intensely individualistic. The diffuse structure of racing in this country, combined with the twin British obsessions of privacy and property, have meant that racing stables have developed into little, and sometimes not so little, empires. Trainers are traditionally referred to as the 'Master' of their establishments (an archaism that still retains a good deal of meaning in some yards, where the stentorian bark of 'the guv'nor' is designed to strike fear into lads and visitors alike). Even at those places in Britain where trainers are grouped together, at the traditional training centres of Newmarket, Lambourn, Malton, Middleham and Epsom, each individual yard is still very much a private domain, with its own peculiar character, history and time-honoured set of rituals.

Although some counties, like Berkshire and Suffolk, have greater concentrations of racing stables than others, the distribution of racing stables in Britain is genuinely nationwide: there

A familiar sight on the motorways of Britain: Jack Berry's much-travelled horsebox.

are yards in every county in England and in most districts of Scotland and Wales, apart from the extreme celtic fringe. Despite the closure of many racecourses during the last twenty years, the advent of all weather gallops and the improvement of the road network has increased the viability of far-flung racing stables in seemingly inauspicious surroundings. Most jockeys and trainers complain about Britain's clogged up roads, but before the building of the M6, Jack Berry's remarkable tally of winners would not have been possible, at least not from a base in North Lancashire, where the only flat racecourse within a radius of fifty miles is Haydock.

In making the selection of the forty stables in this book (there are over 700 racing stables in Britain) I have attempted to reflect this geographical diversity. A number of important and interesting yards in the racing centres of Newmarket and Upper Lambourn have, as a result, been omitted to avoid repetition. Another important criterion was historical interest. Although I have included two important new yards, in Whitcombe Manor and Jackdaws' Castle, I have attempted to concentrate on those yards with significant racing history.

Finally, it might seem absurd, at a time when racing is widely perceived to be in a state of underfunded crisis, to write a book that glories in the buildings and landscapes of the turf. At the time of writing, many racing yards are, like the bloodstock they house, unsaleable at a decent price, following the dramatic fall in property values. The boom days may indeed be over, but in a recession, I feel it is important to take stock of where real value resides. The funding of racing may be in a mess and where once it was incontrovertible that we had the best racehorses in the world it is now debateable, but one fact cannot be contested and that is, that in Britain, we have undeniably the best and most extraordinarily various facilities for the training of racehorses in the world. It is about time we shouted about it.

FLAT
RACING
STABLES

KINGSCLERE.

IAN BALDING

IAN BALDING DESCRIBES Kingsclere as "the best kept secret in England". Tucked away on the edge of the Hampshire Downs, the estate is a world away from the intensively galloped downland on the other side of the M4. The beautiful old yard, laid out by John Porter in the mid-nineteenth century and the superlative Watership Down gallops, are among the most precious treasures of the English turf and yet few people have seen them.

Master of all that he surveys, Kingsclere's new proprietor, Ian Balding, casts an eye over second lot.

Despite being Hampshire born and bred and from a racing family, Ian Balding had never visited Kingsclere, until one day he was invited to ride work on a point-to-pointer belonging to Peter Makin's mother, who had the use of a gallop adjacent to the Kingsclere gallops, which is still known as "Mrs Makin's". The young amateur rider's first brush with the Kingsclere estate was not a happy one: "I was tearing over the top of the hill much too fast when suddenly I came across Peter Hastings' Kingsclere string crossing the road. I had two options: I could either screech to a halt and scare everything to death, or just keep going, so I kept going". Despite this inauspicious introduction, Peter Hastings was sufficiently enamoured of the young Balding's abilities as a horseman, that he later invited him to become his assistant trainer. Balding accepted but thought of the arrangment as short term, because at the time he had intended setting up a jumping stable with his elder brother Toby, the idea being that he would ride most of the horses himself.

Tragically, only three months into the job at Kingsclere, Peter Hastings died, presenting the 25 year old Balding with the opportunity of taking charge of perhaps England's most famous racing stable. "It was a daunting prospect", he remembers, "but also extremely exciting". Security of tenure was a worry, particularly as tax problems meant that the Hastings-Bass family were forced to sell the estate. Enter Kingsclere's saviour, the Canadian industrialist, John McDougald, one of the yard's longstanding owners, who was contacted by the worried

Park House in the days of John Porter.
(Racing Illustrated)

young trainer and who agreed to help out by buying the estate. A long term tenancy was arranged, much to Ian Balding's relief, with an option to purchase at any time. At the time, such an option seemed a long way off but it has always been Ian Balding's ambition to be able to pass on the estate to his son and, at the beginning of the 1992 season, the option was finally exercised.

Appropriately enough, it was a similar tale of benign patronage that first launched Park House, Kingsclere as a racing stable. Inevitably, given the scale of the estate, the yard's history has been a story of a succession of rich men as well as trainers. The first of these was Sir Joseph Hawley, a colourful figure of the Victorian turf, who kept strict control of stable administration and the placing of horses, employing trainers largely as glorified stud grooms. After running a very successful stable in converted farm buildings at nearby Cannons Heath for many years, with a young John Porter employed as his private trainer, Hawley built a new yard at Kingsclere in 1867. It was considerably smaller than the present yard and the trainer's status was reflected in the tiny cottage in which he was expected to live.

Mill Reef's statue, in the yard named after him.

Park House today, essentially unchanged in a century.

Eight years later, Hawley died, generously including a clause in his will giving his young trainer the option to purchase the estate for £4,000, half what it had originally cost. The ambitious Porter, who was rapidly becoming the leading trainer of his day, exercised the option and set about transforming the yard into a model of its type. In his autobiography, he describes the process: "I was very anxious that the architect should embody in his designs the ideas I had formed regarding the requirements of a racing stable; so when I was convalescent (Porter had been struck down with typhoid) I obtained a drawing board, T-square, pencil and paper and set to work to prepare some plans". Porter did an excellent job; more than a century later, the old yard works as well as ever. It has a lasting beauty that derives from being utterly functional: spacious, airy boxes; excellent drainage and no slippery surfaces. Such is the air of permanence and solidity about the place that it seems probable that it will still be working perfectly in another hundred years.

Another legacy from the nineteenth century are the superb gallops laid out by Porter on Watership Down. His famous Derby gallop, a winding valley gallop cutting through the undulations of the Downs out of sight of the ever present touts, survives today, albeit in slightly altered form. With the benefits of modern technology, Ian Balding has removed a large bank which used to cut across "just as they were getting going" according to Kingsclere's new master.

Despite training 23 classic winners, including such legendary horses as Ormonde and Flying Fox, for some of the most notable people in the land, including the Prince of Wales, Porter's thoughts in retirement reveal the perennial insecurity of a trainer's lot. "Experience had proved to me that the emoluments I received as a trainer merely provided sufficient to live upon. There was no surplus to put in the bank. Any money I have saved has come to me in the form of presents from my patrons and as a result of fortunate speculations in bloodstock".

Even before Porter's retirement in 1905, the estate cost so much to maintain that it had been reconstituted as 'Kingsclere Ltd', a syndicate involving the Dukes of Portland and Westminster. After Porter's retirement, they employed William Waugh as their trainer, but despite sending out two further classic winners in Troutbeck and Winkipop, the glory days of Porter were never recaptured. A fallow period ensued between 1919 and 1934, when training resumed under the control of Fred Butters, younger brother of the Aga Khan's trainer, who added to the Kingsclere roll of honour by training Mid-day Sun to win the Derby of 1937. Two years later, war broke out and Kingsclere's gallops were silent once more.

John 'Jonna' Holly, Kingsclere's long-serving gallops man.

After the war, during which time American soldiers had been stationed in Park House, the former jump jockey Evan Williams took out a licence to train at Kingsclere. Previously Williams had been secretary to Ivor Anthony at Wroughton, the stable Aubrey Hastings had made famous by training no less than four Grand National winners. Hastings' son Peter, after learning his trade under Ivor Anthony at Wroughton for six years, bought Kingsclere in the early 1950s, and took out a license to train there in 1953 on Williams' retirement.

The Wroughton connection survives today. Ian Balding married Peter Hastings' daughter, Emma, who, along with William Hastings-Bass, now Lord Huntingdon, grew up at Kingsclere in the 1950s. Ivor Anthony, the old Wroughton trainer, retired to Kingsclere and Emma Balding remembers him well: "He used to invite us to tea at his house and taught me to play gin rummy. He was very active and was always out with the horses on his old cob".

The present era has seen a considerable expansion and development of the Kingsclere estate under Ian Balding's stewardship. The bedrock of any racing yard is always its patrons and in this department, Ian Balding and Kingsclere have been very fortunate. In addition to the patronage of the Queen, Balding benefited from the Hastings family's association with Paul Mellon, who has remained loyal to the stable ever since. It was one of Paul Mellon's horses, of course, that provided Balding with the kind of early boost of which every aspirant trainer dreams. Mill Reef is remembered at Kingsclere today with his own yard, built around a fine sculpture of himself.

Ironically, the career of Paul Mellon's legendary colt came to an end on the same gallops that had underpinned his early development; even the perfect springy turf on Watership Down could not prevent Mill Reef from breaking his leg one late summer morning during a routine strong canter. Such is fate, and racing.

Racing silks in the Kingsclere colours room,
impromptu scene of Mill Reef's life-saving operation.

PAST TRAINERS:
John Porter; William Waugh; Fred Butters; Evan Williams;
Captain P.R.H. Hastings-Bass; Colonel Dick Poole

NOTABLE HORSES:
Blue Gown; Pero Gomez; Isonomy; Shotover; St Blaise; Farewell;
Paradox; Ormonde; Perdita II; La Fleche; Throstle; Sainfoin;
Common; Flying Fox; La Roche; Troutbeck; Winkipop; Clarissimus;
Mid-day Sun; Supreme Court; Silly Season; Mill Reef;
Silver Fling; Forest Flower; Dashing Blade;
Selkirk; Lochsong

OWNERS:
HM The Queen; HM Queen Elizabeth the Queen Mother;
Paul Mellon; George Strawbridge; Sheikh Mohammed; J.C. Smith;
Baron Oppenheim; R.P.B. Michaelson; Simon Berry;
Mrs M.A. Rae Smith: D.H. Back; Miss A.V. Hill; Michael Gauge;
David Myers; Mrs Michael Wates; Nigel Harris; Mrs Page;
Jerrard Williamson; Woodhaven Stud.

Fitzroy House, Newmarket.

Michael Bell

The Fitzroy House stable, on Newmarket's Racecourse side, can lay claim to be one of the town's most significant yards. It is by no means the biggest or most imposing of the town's sixty or so racing stables, but its associations with a string of racing's most colourful and influential characters make it a notable landmark of the twentieth century turf.

The first of these was Robert Standish Sievier, a rakish gambler and adventurer, reputedly born in the back of a London hansom cab, whose 'career' on the turf can be seen as a series of skirmishes, both with authority and the bookmaking fraternity. His association with Fitzroy House began in 1912 with a winning bet and ended, ten years later, with a spectacular loser.

Sievier had made his first real impact on the British racing scene at the turn of the century, when he paid a record 10,000 guineas (the proceeds of a number of succesful gambles) for a yearling called Sceptre at the dispersal sale of the Duke of Westminster's horses. It proved an inspired purchase: Sceptre turned out to be a genuine candidate for the racehorse of the century, winning both Guineas in addition to the Oaks and the St Leger. The consensus of opinion among turf historians is that Sceptre achieved what she did despite Bob Sievier, who, in conjunction with an inexperienced American assistant, subjected the horse to a gruelling schedule, beginning bizarrely (for a potential classic filly) with the Lincoln, and taking in, incredibly, every British classic of the season, in addition to a trip to France for the Grand Prix and appearances at Goodwood and Ascot. Despite all the filly's wins that year, Sievier contrived to lose money on her, backing her heavily on the few occasions that she was beaten, most notably in the Derby.

A lot of responsibility on young shoulders, Fitzroy House's young trainer, Michael Bell.

A decade later, Sievier's luck had changed. Warlingham's win in the Cesarewitch of 1912 was one of the great gambling manoeuvres of all time, a strategem planned from the moment the horse was bought out of a lowly seller at Newbury. With a fraction of the money that he won on Warlingham, Sievier purchased Fitzroy House, the yard from which the Hon. George Lambton's younger brother, Freddie, had commenced training the year before.

Sievier was granted a training licence, despite having been warned off for unspecified offences some years previously. Sievier had many enemies in the more respectable racing circles, an unpopularity exacerbated by his publication of a scurrilous racing paper called *The Winning*

Birds' eye view of the core of the main yard, built over a century ago.

Post, a kind of *Private Eye* of the turf. For seven seasons, Sievier combined training with editing until in 1919, his licence was withdrawn because it was felt that such a combination was unethical and not in racing's best interests.

Sievier continued to have horses in training and to gamble spectactularly. The latter was to prove his downfall; chasing losses, he staked everything on a horse called Monarch in the Victoria Cup of 1922. It lost - by a short head - and within two years, Fitzroy House had been sold and *The Winning Post* was no more.

Fitzroy's next owner was a man of an altogether different stamp: Sir Victor Sassoon, the first of a succession of wealthy men to shape the stable's future. At the same time as the purchase of Fitzroy House in 1925, Sir Victor began spending huge sums on the purchase of horses, setting up his friend, the vet and amateur rider, J.H. Crawford, as his private trainer. Sassoon would go on to own a clutch of classic winners but the nearest he got with Crawford and the Fitzroy House team was with Hot Night, who came second in Call Boy's Derby of 1927.

Sir Victor's successor as patron of the Fitzroy House stable was his big rival in the sales rings of the time, the then Aga Khan, who transferred his entire string from the Whatcombe stable of R.C. 'Dick' Dawson after a public row in 1931. The recipient of this benefaction was the well-travelled 53 year old Frank Butters, who had set himself up as a private trainer for the first time the previous year, after spells in Austria, Italy and at Stanley House, where he had been private trainer to Lord Derby.

The Aga's horses put Fitzroy House on the map. For the next twenty years, barring the

Head lad, David Bradley and Totally Unique return from a midwinter workout.

interruption of the war, when the Aga lived in neutral Switzerland, barely a major race went by without a Fitzroy House runner in the famous 'green and chocolate hoops, chocolate cap' colours. One of the most remarkable feats of those years was one of the earliest. In the St Leger of 1932, Frank Butters saddled four of the Aga Khan's horses: Udaipur; Firdaussi; Taj Kasra and Dastur. Firdaussi won, Dastur was second, Udaipur was fourth and Taj Kasra fifth. Although the majority of the horses in the yard belonged to the Aga, Butters continued to train for other longstanding owners (the 1934 Oaks winner, Light Brocade, was owned by the Earl of Durham) with the consequence that the Fitzroy House string, numbering around 70 horses, was among the largest in the country. The best horses Butters trained for the Aga were undoubtedly Bahram and Mahmoud, who won the Derby in successive years in 1935 and '36. Mahmoud, who was by the Whatcombe-trained sire, Blenheim, out of Mah Mahal, a grandaughter of Mumtaz Mahal, the flying filly of Whatcombe, was one of only four greys to win the Derby.

After Butters was knocked off his bicycle by a truck outside the gates of Fitzroy House in 1949, an accident which rendered him unfit to train, Marcus Marsh was appointed as the Aga Khan's trainer. In a cruel twist of fate, Butters left behind him a spectacular legacy for his successor in the form of a champion crop of two year olds, including the next year's 2,000 Guineas winner, Palestine. With the backing of the richest man in the world, Marsh followed this up by becoming champion trainer in 1952, winning both the Derby and the St Leger of that year with Tulyar, who was by Tehran, an earlier Fitzroy House-trained horse of the Aga's.

Despite his success, in a move that would be echoed by his grandson decades later, the Aga decided in the same year that the rewards of racing in England were insufficient and transferred the majority of his horses to France. Marsh's contract was not renewed, but the success of previous seasons enabled Marsh to stay on at Fitzroy House for another nine years. During that time, the stable's fortunes inevitably waned and by the time the yard was sold to Sir Robin McAlpine in 1962, there were barely a dozen horses in training at Fitzroy House.

Sir Robin McAlpine installed John Waugh as his private trainer. John Waugh, who now manages Sir Robin's Wyck Hall Stud, comes from a very distinguished and longstanding family of trainers, and is the grandson of Richard Waugh, who trained for Kaiser Wilhelm at Graditz before the First World War. Fitzroy House had fallen into a state of disrepair by the early 1960s and Sir Robin set about a considerable programme of rebuilding and improvement. Training at Fitzroy House during the 1960s was a very much reduced affair, with a maximum of 25 horses. Classic success was never forthcoming but the yard pulled off a number of good victories in handicaps with horses like Pardoner and Apiarian.

The fillies' block: Lovealoch looks on demurely.

Since McAlpine's private stable was closed down in 1970, Fitzroy House has had one further patron of note, in the shape of Captain Marcos Lemos, who bought the yard in 1982 and spent a considerable sum of money on its refurbishment and extension. On the training side, Frankie Durr began his training career at the yard in 1979 with a bang, sending out a number of good winners in his first year, including the speedy Ahonoora, who won the William Hill Sprint Championship and who is now proving a major success at stud.

Unlike many of the yard's trainers in the past, Fitzroy House's present incumbent, Michael Bell, is very much a public trainer, with an impressive tally of owners ready to sing his praises. Prince Fahd Salman has continued to support his principal trainer Paul Cole's former assistant, as does father-in-law, Alan Lillingston, owner of the Mount Coote Stud in Ireland, but most of Bell's owners have a single horse or a share in one, making the number of horses in training at Fitzroy House today an impressive achievement in itself, particularly in the depths of a recession. Remarkably, there are now more horses than at any time in the past, including the glory days of the 1930s. Despite the absence of a major patron, Fitzroy House's long term future seems assured, given such energetic and youthful stewardship.

OWNERS:

Prince Fahd Salman; Lady d'Avigdor-Goldsmid; Jocelyn Hambro; Alan Lillingston; David Thompson; Sir Thomas Pilkington; Yucel Birol; Brian Cooper

PAST TRAINERS:

J. Torterolo; Hon.F. Lambton; Bob Sievier; J.H. Crawford; Frank Butters; Marcus Marsh; John Waugh; Peter Robinson; Frankie Durr; Ray Hutchinson

NOTABLE HORSES:

Royal Bucks; Hot Night; Lord Bill; Bahram; Udaipur; Firdaussi; Dastur; Light Brocade; Turkhan; Tehran; Mahmoud; Migoli; Masaka; Palestine; Tulyar; Ahonoora; Pass the Peace; A-to-Z

Moss Side Racing Stables, Cockerham.

Jack Berry

The North Lancashire village of Cockerham is now firmly established on the racing map. In an area more used to the grazing of sheep and the rearing of cattle, Jack Berry's ever-burgeoning yard must have seemed something of a cuckoo in the nest to bewildered locals. From very modest beginnings, the small, semi-derelict farm on the other side of the caravan park has been completely transformed into the North of England's leading training establishment.

Standing on flat, low-lying land about a mile away from the village, the entire complex only becomes visible in the last few hundred yards before arrival. It is an extraordinary sight: the hedgerows and small fields of surrounding farms give way to a huge oblong of land filled with what looks, at first glance, like a racecourse, minus the grandstand. Acres of white painted running rail, grass and all weather gallops, immaculate starting stalls and even a red telephone box add up to a passable mirage of a sixtieth racecourse.

Jack Berry on board the yard's token jumper, No More the Fool.

When the aspiring trainer first visited the site twenty years ago, in the company of his then business partner, James Kearsley, he immediately saw through the dereliction of the farm buildings, to the potential of the land itself. "When we were at Doncaster, it was hard work because the ground used to get so baked up in summer. Here, the ground is so good in summer, it's a pleasure to fall off, a really good cushion".

Jack Berry's ideal yard had been taking shape for years when, as a freelance jump jockey riding work for any number of small northern stables, he picked up "all manner of ideas here and there". These inchoate plans took shape for the first time in the form of pencil doodles in the unlikely surroundings of Lincoln Hospital, where Jack was laid up after a bad fall at Market Rasen. In a typically graphic passage from his immensely readable autobiography, *It's Tougher at the Bottom*, Jack describes his dream yard in graphic detail, from the division of staff into work riders and grooms, right down to the plumbing and the colour of the paintwork.

Exactly as J.Berry envisaged it:
the main yard at Moss Side.

With characteristic singlemindedness - "Once I get an idea, I'll go through fire and water seeing it through" - and serious amounts of 'hard graft', Berry eventually got exactly what he wanted, although the original 21-box yard is now dwarfed by subsequent development. There are now 114 boxes - all filled - in the yard. Only the avant garde, American-style staff arrangements have yet to be put into practice: "It'll only be a matter of time before that happens if racing ever becomes more centralised". Despite the fulfillment of those early dreams, complacency is not a word to be found in the Berry vocabulary.

"The moment you start thinking that you've got where you wanted to be, that's when you'll go down. You've got to remain ambitious and forceful". And, beneath the friendly, chirpy exterior, it is not hard to see that Jack Berry is very much a driven character, always seeking after new challenges. Not for him, the relaxed demeanour of the man of leisure. "My old guv'nor, Charlie Hall was far more of a gentleman than me. He was a nice man and a good trainer but he wouldn't have had to go and graft. It's a different game today; if I was as gentlemanly as Charlie Hall, I wouldn't survive".

In these recessionary times, it is fear as much as ambition that drives Berry on. "The kind of people whose businesses are going down all over the place are exactly the ones who'd have a horse with me. It would be tragic if this great industry were allowed to go the way of the motorbike and cotton industry. Nobody really believed that they would ever go but they did. At the moment, I'm trying to develop the racing club side of things. With them, the financial commitment involved in having a horse is not so great. They're good for the game, too, getting more and more people interested in ownership".

It is obvious that Jack Berry was tailor-made for this aspect of modern training. With his red shirt and characteristically shaped trilby, he is a fixture on the racecourse and a beacon for the kind of gossipers and autograph hunters, who assume an easy acquaintanceship purely because someone is in the public eye. Unlike many successful people, Jack has never become blasé and always has a kind word for a fan, with the consequence that he has become something of a pied piper of the racing world, selling the game at open days and charity dos whenever commitments allow.

Constant reminders of success. The yard has run out of space for its winners' plaques.

Moss Side Racing Stables itself performs a similar public relations role. As well as being a well-run professional yard, it is also a beautifully presented public showcase. Everywhere you look there are tiny reminders of the Moss Side team's phenomenal success, in the shape of prettily painted plaques recording each victory, with the name of the horse, track and date painstakingly recorded. Not surprisingly, in recent recordbreaking seasons, this proved a tall order. "An old boy in the village used to do them for me at £3 a go, but with all the winners we'd been having, it all got a bit much for him. He couldn't cope with that many!"

Despite such innovatory touches, Moss Side is also a traditionally run yard, with all the conventional attention to detail associated with a top class racing stable. It is immaculately clean and tidy and like all really good yards, exudes an air of quiet efficiency. Considering the sheer scale of the operation, there is a remarkable absence of clutter and noise. At the end of a morning's work, when the only sign of life comes from the mechanical sqeaking of a couple of horsewalkers exercising a dozen young horses, the old cliche 'running like clockwork' seems particularly appropriate.

OWNERS:

Sir Piers Bengough; R. Sangster; J. Clayton; Lord Mostyn; William Robertson; Richard Jinks; Mr E. St.George; Palacegate Corporation; Laurel Leisure Ltd; R. Peebles; M. Grubb; David Abell; F. Dunne; Yahya Nasib; R. Leah; A. Shelton; N. Harper; P.E.T. Chandler; J. Nixon; Peter Hilton.

PAST TRAINERS

None

NOTABLE HORSES:

O.I.Oyston; So Careful; Distinctly North; Paris House

Kingstone Warren, Oxfordshire.

Henry Candy

High on the summer gallops at White Horse Hill, eight hundred and fifty feet above sea level, it feels like the top of the world. The spine of Britain's racing downland, the Ridgeway, stretches away to Avebury and Beckhampton in the west and to West Ilsley and the Chilterns in the east, like the vertebrae of some vast sleeping dragon. On a clear day, half of England can be scanned in one panoramic swoop.

The man fortunate enough to have cause to survey this glorious scene day after day is Henry Candy, who has spent most of his life on the Kingstone Warren estate he inherited from his father, Derrick Candy. Quite apart from the views, what really distinguishes this spot lies in the more immediate foreground and the middle distance because the gallops at Kingstone Warren are one of the marvels of the British turf: 1,000 acres of the most perfect downland grass in the country, first laid out by the Earl of Craven in the 1730s. Between them, the gallops at Scary Hill; Kingstone Warren Bottom and White Horse Hill contain just about every conceivable variant of distance and incline.

On top of the world: the Candys watching work at Kingstone Warren.

The summer gallops are of particular interest.
At the height of midsummer, in the middle of a heatwave, without the benefit of peat moss or watering, the grass on these unique gallops remains as soft and springy as a carpet. This small agricultural miracle is the result of a rare type of downland grass, sheep fescue, which possesses an extraordinary surface root system that enables it to thrive on the most unpromisingly hard and flinty soil. Even in the harshest of dry summers, there is always a good covering of this remarkable grass. Unsurprisingly, as the ground dries out elsewhere, there are requests to make use of this extraordinary natural resource but, sequestered away as it is from the hustle and bustle of neighbouring Lambourn, and shielded from major roads by extensive farmland, the Kingstone Warren estate is relatively little known, even to locals. Perhaps, in a sense, the summer gallops at Kingstone Warren are almost too good. Given the prevalent firm ground conditions on most British racecourses these days, particularly in the height of summer, it must be quite a shock for an inexperienced horse, used to the luxuriant springiness of White Horse Hill turf, to meet the kind of worn-out, rock hard ground generally available today.

When Derrick Candy first came to Kingstone Warren after the war (before the outbreak of hostilities he had trained in a small way, largely for members of his family at Childrey) it was very different from the extensive set-up that greets the eye today. A small racing yard with

Up to the gallops in the early morning mist.

barely twenty boxes was tagged onto a medium-sized farm belonging to another tenant. In the interwar years, a succession of small National Hunt trainers had leased the yard. The highpoint of Kingstone Warren's early career came in 1938, when Roderic Gubbins trained his own horse, the nine year old grey, Our Hope, to win the Champion Hurdle. All the gallops that now distinguish the estate as one of Britain's great private training establishments belonged at that time to the neighbouring Seven Barrows yard, made famous in the 1920s and '30s by Harry Cottrill. According to Henry Candy, Kingstone Warren "very much played second fiddle".

The Kingstone Warren estate as it is presently constituted began to take shape in 1958, when its then owners, the ill-fated Craven family, who owned just about everything in the valley, were forced, through death duties and other misfortunes, to sell off their estates lock, stock and barrel. The farm and racing yard at Kingstone Warren were lumped in with the neighbouring Seven Barrows estate, in a single lot. At a time of depressed land values, Derrick Candy just managed to scrape together enough money to buy the lot. Henry Candy remembers his father asking him, in which house he would prefer to live. "Like all young boys, I wanted to remain where I was, and I must say I have never changed my mind".

Soon afterwards, evidently deciding that young Henry's advice was worth heeding, and enjoying the freedom of his newfound status of landlord, Derrick Candy set about changing the boundaries of the two estates to Kingstone Warren's advantage, reapportioning the 1,000 acres of gallops that formerly went with Seven Barrows to Kingstone Warren. The latter was no longer the poor relation.

Buffered against the outside world by its extensive acreage, the estate today seems a charmed place removed from the harsh economic realities that beset racing lives elsewhere. Appearances can be deceptive but to a certain extent this is true of Kingstone Warren, a fact reflected in Henry Candy's relaxed approach to training. Horses on the estate are never rushed for short term gain for the simple fact that their owners do not require them to be. As Henry Candy puts it "I train mostly for established owner/breeders who don't perhaps feel the pinch as much as some and therefore there is no need to rush horses along".

The many and various gallops at Kingstone Warren contain every conceivable incline.

Another corollary of this kind of regime is the continuity of bloodlines. The present crop is liberally sprinkled with horses whose dams, granddams, sires and grandsires have themselves been in training on the very same gallops. As we ascend the chalky track to the gallops at Kingstone Warren Bottom, a two year old filly, ironically named Gentle

Getting organised before second lot in the main yard.

Moment, rears up and throws her lad into a field of potatoes. As she gallops off, bucking and kicking, Mr Candy remembers her mother as "the biggest bit of baggage imaginable. She never wore hind shoes as she was always liable to kick". Later on, watching second lot circling in the shade of a picturesque clump of beech trees - the shallow rooted tree of the chalk downlands - half their number seem to be related to Master Willie, High Line or any of the other bloodlines that run through the string, a familiarity that obviously gives their trainer a lot of pleasure.

It is also useful: the now almost veteran Henry Candy can recall more than twenty five seasons at Kingstone Warren as assistant and trainer and is able, therefore, to draw upon an invaluable library of equine family histories to deal with any training or temperament problem relating to the latest branch of the family tree to arrive.

On a summer's day up on the Downs, with the larks singing and young horses beginning to show promise on the gallops, Henry Candy has to be one of the luckiest men in England.

PAST TRAINERS:

W. Raisin; A. Gordon; E.J.R. Bennett; Roderic Gubbins; Derrick Candy

PAST ASSISTANTS:

Capt.T.Forster; M Blanshard; M. Usher; N. Holden; R. Phillips

OWNERS:

R. Barnett; Fahd Salman; Major M.G. Wyatt; H.R. Mould; Mrs David Blackburn; P. Goulandris; Lady Sparrow; Lord Chelsea; Lt.Cdr.G.G.Marten; P.A. Deal; J.K. Dale; Capt.M.M.C. Clark; R. Pennant Jones; C.J.R. Trotter; Mrs A. Portman; T.A. Frost; P. Robinson; Mrs C.E. Gross; Mrs E. Roberts; R.S.A. Urquhart; Mrs A. Wright

NOTABLE HORSES:

Our Hope; High Line; Negus; Rhinehart; Song; Time Charter; Master Willie; Wind 'n' Wuthering; Assured; Cut Throat; Pipedreamer; Always Friendly.

Warren Place, Newmarket.

Henry Cecil

Warren Place is special. Both by virtue of its situation, tucked away in wooded seclusion at the top of Warren Hill, and its unparalleled record of recent success under Sir Noel Murless and Henry Cecil, it stands apart from the other yards in the town.

In pre-hard hat days, the legendary Sir Noel Murless on the Heath in his customary trilby. (photo courtesy the late Lady Murless)

The story of Warren Place begins in the autumn of 1925, with the victories of Masked Marvel in the Cambridgeshire and Forsetti in the Cesarewitch (the kudos of both races was considerably greater at the time than now). Both were trained by Sam Darling Junior, eldest son of the Beckhampton trainer and brother of Fred: a feat that has never been achieved since. Sam might never have been able to match his father and brother in terms of classic success, but made the most of the material that came his way and rarely entertained an angel unawares, with the consequence that he became that rarest of creatures: a wealthy gambler.

Warren Place is a lasting monument to Sam Darling's worldly success. The first stage in its development was Darling's purchase of Warren Towers, an imposing property, which presided over the training grounds on Bury Side like a latterday King's Chair. Darling immediately saw the potential of the surrounding land for development as a racing stable. Although Newmarket as a training centre had broken out of the restricted confines of its nineteenth century borders with the construction of the spacious new yards along the Bury Road, there was still a lack of privacy, not to mention style and individuality about the existing stock of training establishments.

With the construction of Warren Place, Sam Darling and his design-minded wife Thora changed all that. Its construction caused quite a stir in the locality; the extent of the comings and goings earned the burgeoning site the nickname 'Harvey Nichols'. (Liberty's might have been more appropriate, as the mock-Tudor trainer's house bears more than a passing resemblance to the half-timbered Regent Street store).

Maples were the principal contractors and nominally responsible for the design, although surviving members of the Darling clan, including Sam Darling's daughter, Betty, maintain that Thora Darling had the final say. In scale and style, Warren Place was quite unlike the generally

The elegant classical lines of the yard at Warren Place were modelled on an Italian original.

modest trainers' houses attached to the principal Newmarket yards. In size, it was more like the kind of house that had hitherto been the temporary racing residences of aristocracy, a fact that was also reflected in its architectural character, which was that of a grandiose hunting lodge.

Throughout its early life, Warren Place had a glamorous aura. When Elizabeth (Betty) Darling held her 21st birthday party at the house soon after it was built, no less a star than Fred Astaire (later to be best man at her wedding to Jack Leach) danced for the assembled company, only to slip on the religiously polished parquet flooring. The horses, too, enjoyed considerable luxury; no expense was spared in the construction of their stabling. Betty Darling remembers her father visiting Frank Butters, a member of that great itinerant training family later to return to England and become the Aga Khan's principal trainer, who was then training in Italy, and being so impressed that he used an Italian stable yard as a model for Warren Place.

Fittingly, Warren Place's next owner was royal, the Maharajah of Baroda, who had already made a spectacular impact on the postwar racing scene by paying a record price for a yearling (Sayajirao) in 1945. The year after, he installed Sam Armstrong as his trainer at Warren Place, dividing up the house and continuing to live in its principal apartments himself. This arrangement did not last long. The Maharani decided that she wanted the entire house and, rather than live away from the yard, the Armstrong string moved down the hill to St Gatien. The gap proved impossible to fill and Warren Place became something of a white elephant for a number of years, until the arrival of the man who would make its name famous throughout the racing world.

When the Murless family arrived at Warren Place, it had been empty for four years. "The gardens were like a hayfield", according to Lady Murless, who remembers her late husband arranging the transportation of the entire string from Beckhampton to Newmarket in one day. "We had a few runners at Newmarket at one of the autumn meetings, who remained there and the rest came lock, stock and barrel by road. The entire staff slept at Beckhampton one night and Warren Place the next".

Although Murless had achieved notable success at both Hambleton and Beckhampton, it was at Warren Place that he really laid his claim to greatness. After Sir Gordon Richards' retirement in 1954, the young Lester Piggott became stable jockey (with no less a jockey than Geoff Lewis as a lightweight No.2) and a star-studded era began. Unlike some of the names on the equine roll of honour that soon recede into the ether, the names of the horses that Sir Noel Murless trained over the next 21 years retain their power. Horses like Crepello, Petite Etoile and St Paddy live on in the memory.

Sir Noel Murless is remembered by those who knew him as a gentleman and a complete professional. There was nothing miraculous about his method, according to Lady Murless, he was simply a supremely dedicated and knowledgeable horseman who always put the interests of his horses first, regardless of public pressure. He would feed a carrot to all his horses (quite a feat at his peak) at evening stables and was a believer in traditional feed: Australian oats and Canadian hay, a policy adopted by his successor Henry Cecil.

For Cecil, the experience of taking over at Warren Place after some time in the purpose-built Marriott yard in the Hamilton Road, was daunting but liberating. "I've always loved it. It's just far enough out of Newmarket to be quiet and peaceful and compared with most other Newmarket yards it's spacious". The young Henry Cecil already had considerable experience of life in a big Newmarket yard, having acted as assistant to his stepfather, Captain Sir Cecil Boyd Rochfort for a number of years at Freemason Lodge. Then in the twilight of his career, 'the Captain', as he was universally known, had 'mellowed' according to his stepson. "I always found him a terrific person to work for and he gave me quite a lot of responsibility. I was aware of his reputation but he was always very good to me". Along with Sir Noel Murless, Cecil counts Boyd Rochfort as the principal influence on his early career. "I wouldn't perhaps give my horses such a long exercise as he did because times have moved on, but he was very patient, which I hope has rubbed off".

Gwen Murless and daughter Julie at the leaded windows of the house nicknamed 'Harvey Nichols'. (photograph, courtesy the late Lady Murless)

Now in his eighteenth season in charge at Warren Place, Cecil has established his own pattern. With the longstanding backing of a number of wealthy and understanding owner breeders, Warren Place has remained the yardstick against which other aspirants to the title of top stable have to measure themselves. Quite apart from the tally of classics and group race victories, it is the stable's consistently high strike rate that takes the eye. Maintaining a rate above 30 per cent, while others struggle to reach 20 per cent is a remarkable testament to the exacting standards of the yard.

In 1976, there were approximately 80 boxes at Warren Place. There are now 140, a

A sleepy midday scene at Warren Place.

reflection of the 'numbers game' that training at 'headquarters' has become. The Master of Warren Place believes that the place has now reached its full capacity. "I wouldn't want to train any more than I've got but it's a fact of modern training life that you're more likely to win a war if you've got an army".

PAST TRAINERS:
Sam Darling; Sam Armstrong; Sir Noel Murless

OWNERS:
Lord Howard de Walden; Sheikh Mohammed; Prince Faisal; Prince Khalid Al Saud; K. Abdulla; Sir David Wills; Cliveden Stud; L. Marinopoulos; S.S. Niarchos; R. Sangster; S.Khaled; Charles.H.Wacker III; A.L.R.Morton; Mrs Mark Burrell; Q.Irshid; Angus Dundee Ltd; Stephen Crown; Mrs H.G.Cambanis; Michael Poland; Ivan Allan.

PAST ASSISTANTS:
John Gosden; Luca Cumani; Willie Jarvis; William Hastings-Bass

NOTABLE HORSES:
My Babu; Sayajirao; Crepello; Carrozza; Petite Etoile; St Paddy; Aurelius; Aunt Edith; Royal Palace; Fleet; Busted; Caergwrle; Lupe; Connaught; Lorenzaccio; Magic Flute; Altesse Royale; Mysterious; J.O.Tobin Le Moss; Fairy Footsteps; One in a Million; Light Cavalry; Ardross; Oh So Sharp; Slip Anchor; Reference Point; Kris; Diminuendo; Old Vic; Buckskin; Gunner B; Indian Skimmer; Belmez; Commander-in Chief

MANTON, WILTSHIRE.

PETER CHAPPLE-HYAM

MANTON IS ONE of the enchanted places of the English turf. For more than a century, the beauty and extent of its downland gallops have cast their spell over some of the most distinguished names, human and equine, to have been associated with the sport of horse racing. The estate's most famous son, Alec Taylor Junior, the 'Wizard of Manton', became so attached to the place that he hardly ever left it, except to go racing. One of his latterday successors, Barry Hills, once said that in all his time at Manton, he only visited the neighbouring town of Marlborough twice - for a haircut. Even on the briefest of visits to this extraordinary patch of Wiltshire downland, its allure is palpable.

On the long narrow road up to the estate from the outskirts of Marlborough, Manton reveals itself only gradually: a running rail glimpsed through a hedgerow and a strip of gallop standing out on a distant hillside. It is only after half a dozen such sightings, all in different directions that one realises the sheer scale of the place. It is simply too big to take in at a single glance.

Manton House Yard today is as imposing as ever but is now used as an isolation area for sick horses.

When Manton was first created in the late 1860s, the gabled grandeur of the Manton House Yard provided the first trainer, Alec Taylor Senior, with a single focal point for his training operation. This imposing block survives intact, but Manton House Yard is nowadays complemented by both the Barton House Yard, originally built to house yearlings but developed now into a fully fledged racing yard, and the ultra-modern Astor complex laid out by Michael Dickinson on a gentle slope adjacent to the old yard.

In the days of Taylor, Lawson and, more latterly, George Todd, Manton was a large training establishment but by no means the largest in the country. Joe Lawson had an average of 50 in training at any one time and his successor, George Todd, anywhere between 40 and 60. In its entirety, Manton today stretches across 2,300 acres of downland (of which 500 are exclusively devoted to racing) connected by 6 miles of private stone-dust road. From the Barton Yard near Marlborough on one side of the estate, to the furthest extent of the famous Derby gallop (there are eleven separate gallops in all) on the other, is a distance of about three miles on the estate roads. Even in Alec Taylor's day, when the estate was constituted differently, the gallops were far flung. *Country Life's* correspondent wrote of Manton in the 1930s: "Fyfield Downs were their former training ground. Then there were other gallops as far apart as Avebury and Ogbourne, though all part of the Manton establishment".

The sheer extent of the gallops at Manton and its awesome record of racing success - Alec Taylor Junior alone sent out 21 classic winners - have combined to create a lasting aura of mystique about the place that has persisted into the present day. The Whatcombe trainer, Paul Cole, was a pupil assistant to the most recent of the Manton legends, George Todd, who he remembers with something close to awe. "Manton was nothing like it is today in terms of scale, but George Todd was a master of his profession. He was an absolutely brilliant trainer. To him, little things made perfection. He was meticulous about every little detail around the yard in a way that would be impossible today". According to Cole, Todd often had to make the best of limited material. "He was the only person I've ever come across who could actually fashion a horse, with patience and perseverance. He bought Blazing Scent, for instance, out of a seller and it went on to win the Royal Hunt Cup". Such equine alchemy had an understandable by-product in the ring, Todd bringing off some of the most spectacular coups in recent racing history. Even at ground level, betting was taken very seriously at Manton in those days remembers Paul Cole: "some of the lads were shrewd judges and would bet £500-1000 on a horse, which in those days was a lot of money".

In its Victorian heyday, the fifty yard square Manton House Yard was the most palatial in racing.

Since George Todd's day, Manton has been transformed from the place that Cole knew in the 1960s. "Michael Dickinson opened it up and improved it dramatically".Despite the physical improvements, the Manton estate has been newsworthy for very different reasons in recent years. Its rebirth as a training centre under the stewardship of Robert Sangster, had been so fraught with problems that the estate, which had always been referred to by the pools magnate as his 'dream', was rapidly becoming a nightmare.

The failure of both the immensely talented and innovative Michael Dickinson, who attempted to introduce US-style horse-handling (there was a strict demarcation between grooms and work riders rather than the traditional British system of lads 'doing' and riding), and the ultra-professional Barry Hills to last in the Manton hot seat led to the inevitable whisper in the industry that the estate was an unwieldy albatross, an unsaleable jinx that would sour Sangster's love affair with the turf. When Barry Hills' former assistant, Peter Chapple-Hyam, was appointed to the job on Christmas Eve 1990, it was widely thought to be some kind of temporary appointment, prior, perhaps, to a sell-off.

Detail from a bygone era. An ornate gas lamp to illuminate the early morning work.

Manton's new boss, an unassuming and affable young Midlander, brought up at Bishop's Itchington near Warwick and reared on the local National Hunt and point-to-point scene, simply ignored the speculation and set about the business of training. "Nobody told me I was a caretaker. Robert Sangster just said, 'There are twenty eight horses here. I want you to train them and Manton is off the market'. "

Such is racing's perversity, that the smallest string in the yard's recent history, supervised by its least experienced trainer, recorded Manton's best season for some while, culminating in the triumphs of top two year olds, Rodrigo de Triano and Dr Devious, in the Middle Park and the Dewhurst respectively. An excellent start, but who would have believed that such juvenile promise would then be translated into triple classic-winning success? Alec Taylor's Bayardo had done it first in 1908-9, winning the Dewhurst, the Middle Park and then the St Leger the following year, and now, 84 years later, a bit of the old wizardry appeared to be returning to Manton.

For Peter Chapple-Hyam, the first sight of Manton, in the company of his long-time boss, Barry Hills, was overwhelming: "I'd heard all about the place of course but nothing can really prepare you for Manton. I couldn't believe it. It was a complete culture shock". Barry Hills was similarly captivated and set about training in this historic setting with great enthusiasm. "The guv'nor loved the old yard especially and had me and Joe Naughton searching around for bits and pieces left over from George Todd's time for a museum, which was set up in the old yard". Nothing could better illustrate the gulf between Manton past and present than this gruesome collection, which includes a spiked passion killer for excitable colts and weighing room scales upholstered in the skin of the great Bayardo.

The thoroughly modern Chapple-Hyam prefers the custom-built newness of the Dickinson-inspired Astor complex with its neat rows of boxes and two American style barns for the fillies. "The rows of boxes are designed so that when the sun shines, every box gets an equal amount, whereas in a square yard each box only gets it at odd times. I particularly like the barns myself: the fact that there's a constant breeze going through and the horses can enjoy each other's company. I only use the old yard now as an isolation yard - I send badly infected horses down there for seven days - because I find the old boxes a bit depressing and dark for normal purposes. The boxes always seem a bit damp and horses can't see over the tops of the boxes".

Manton's museum. Peter Chapple-Hyam and a set of weighing room scales upholstered in Bayardo's skin!

The gallops on the other hand - all eleven of them - are all fully utilised, albeit at different times of the year. "My time with Barry Hills here has stood me in good stead. I think the problem with Michael Dickinson might have been that he came straight in here and had to get used to them immediately and the gallops here do take some getting used to. They can be very stiff and severe - you can easily ruin a horse on them. I believe in a lot of steady work. You don't have to go fast or far to get them fit. 5 or 6 furlongs as a rule and a few of the older horses might do a mile and a quarter".

Chapple-Hyam's baptism of fire on the Manton gallops was to prepare his two Group One winning two year olds - Rodrigo de Triano and Dr Devious - for their classic races through one of the wettest springs on record. In the very early days of the season, before Rodrigo's reappearance in the Greenham, Chapple-Hyam worked the eventual 2,000 Guineas winner on the Barton gallop, which George Todd had nicknamed "the Dramatic gallop", after the Lincoln winner he prepared on it during a similarly inauspicious early spring. This flat mile and a half stretch was always traditionally good–draining ground, but had been improved further by the perfectionist Michael Dickinson, who introduced a new drainage system.

After the Greenham 'flop', about which Chapple-Hyam was never unduly concerned, the horse was switched to the main 'Clatford gallops' for the build-up to the Guineas. This summer ground is laid out in a huge figure 6 shape on high, gently sloping ground to the north west of the main yard and it is here the majority of the horses' 'bread and butter' work takes place. Eight days before the Guineas, however, Rodrigo was taken, in the company of Lester Piggott for the first time, to Manton's traditional classic trial ground, the famous Derby gallop,

Manton's crowning glory: thoroughbreds in strong work on the downland gallops.

where the Derby winners of seventy years ago were put through their paces ten days before the big race. Despite its name, the Derby gallop bears no resemblance whatsoever to Epsom. It is a straight and tremendously stiff mile, which climbs well over 150 feet over the first seven furlongs.

Chapple-Hyam, who remains endearingly star-struck, recalls the occasion: "It was the first time Lester had been down since George Todd's day. He said he'd never been on the Derby gallop before. We worked him a mile with three pacemakers - Dr Devious, Relentless Pursuit and Berlin Wall - and he went better than anything".

The rest, as they say - and have said at Manton for a while now - is history and, if things continue to progress for the likeable Chapple-Hyam as they have been doing (he is only too well aware that a place like Manton requires success as its lifeblood), the old estate's future looks more assured than it has done since the great days of Todd, Taylor and Lawson.

NOTABLE HORSES:

Sefton; Gang Forward; Craig Miller; Thebais; St Marguerite; Reve D'Or; Lemberg; Rosedrop; Kennymore; Gay Crusader; Sunny Jane; Pogrom; Saucy Sue; Short Story; Love in Idleness; My Dear; Bayuda; Challacombe; Bayardo; Gainsborough; Book Law; Pennycomequick; Orwell; Pay Up; Exhibitionist; Galatea II; Dancing Time; Kingsway; Court Martial; Trelawny; Dramatic; Sodium; Sir Harry Lewis; Glacial Storm; Rodrigo de Triano; Dr Devious

PAST TRAINERS:

Alec Taylor Senior and Junior; Joe Lawson; George Todd; George Peter-Hoblyn; Robert Baker; Michael Dickinson; Barry Hills

PAST ASSISTANTS:

Paul Cole; Peter Chapple-Hyam; Joe Naughton; Chris Wall

OWNERS:

Robert Sangster; Luciano Gaucci; HRH Princess Michael of Kent

Jeremy Tree - Looking Back

Jeremy Tree's memories of Beckhampton stretched back even further than the thirty seven seasons he trained in the racing heart of the Marlborough Downs. Right back to the late 1930s when, as a racing-mad schoolboy, he was taken, for a special treat, to view his uncle, Peter Beatty's Bois Roussel, the Fred Darling-trained Derby winner of 1938. The young would-be trainer had had £1 each way with the school bookie at Eton, at the rewarding odds of 20-1. "A formative experience" said the Master of Beckhampton with a twinkle in the eye in an interview recorded the year before his death.

The only other time Tree visited Beckhampton before embarking on a training career at the yard, was a parentally arranged trip to meet the then retired Fred Darling to seek his advice about becoming a trainer. Unbeknown to the young Tree, the object was to dissuade him. Needless to say, it didn't work.

Although the Beckhampton reins were handed over to long-serving assistant, Roger Charlton, two years ago, Tree lived on in Beckhampton House, cheek by jowl with the bustle of the main yard, a benign, fatherly presence, never proferring but always ready to give advice when called upon and cheering on every Beckhampton runner on a newly installed SIS screen.

A series of minor strokes may have impaired Tree's speed about the yard but not his spirit or interest in racing. Always an erudite man with a broad range of interests outside the game, the former trainer seemed in his element in his library/sitting room, where racing books and newspapers mix easily with bound volumes of the classics and the latest copies of *The Field* and *Country Life*.

Characteristic cigarette holder in hand, the trainer of Known Fact, Rainbow Quest and John Cherry - to name but a few - was as amusing as ever. The news of Lester's acquisition of the 2,000 Guineas ride on Rodrigo de Triano had just emerged in the press, but came as no surprise to Mr Tree. "Some things never change. In the days when Lester used to ride quite a bit for me in the early seventies he used to come down once a year, usually at about the time of the Newbury Spring meeting. It was an occasion I looked forward to with some trepidation. It was fairly obvious that all Lester really wanted to do was to find out what was any good and what he would be prepared to ride and he used to try them all pretty highly. From anyone else it would have been quite unacceptable".

Jeremy Tree's experience of training spans a number of very different eras in British racing, from the relative austerity of the early 1950s through the American-led prosperity of the 1960s, when notable US owners like Charles Englelhard and Jock Whitney had many good horses at Beckhampton, to the arrival of the Arabs in the late 1970s.

Considering the level of Arab involvement in racing today, it is extraordinary that less than fifteen years ago, when retired trainer Humphrey Cottrell suggested that Mr Tree might like to meet an Arab gentleman called Mr Abdulla, the Beckhampton trainer "had no idea who he was". "At the time, I had got used to training for Mr Whitney (the former US Ambassador to the UK for whom Mr Tree trained a number of good horses including Swing Easy amd John Cherry) and didn't really want to start with a lot of new owners. I had even thought of retiring when Mr Whitney eventually gave up, but when Mr Abdulla came along I thought it best not to rock the boat".

In the first batch of yearlings purchased at Keeneland (Tree's first visit to the Kentucky saleroom) for his new Arab patron were subsequent 2,000 Guineas winner Known Fact and the filly Abeer, who won the Queen Mary in 1979. "I think he must have thought this is easy. It would have been quite easy to become spoiled".

Not surprisingly, Mr Tree was a keen advocate of Arab involvement in British racing. "The Arabs have brought a lot of very good horses to this country, which have done nothing but good for our racing and breeding. All the American bred horses for instance that they have introduced have made a tremendous difference. Really what they have done is brought back a lot of the bloodlines that went to the US after the war, when we lost a number of our best horses, such as Tudor Minstrel and Court Martial. So, it's really a question of the best coming back".

Not all the most recent innovations in British racing met with the Tree seal of approval. All weather flat racing in January is not required viewing on the Beckhampton S.I.S screen. "I think it's awful. The way they tear round those tight bends and go like hell, it seems no different from dog racing to me".

Of all the horses that passed through his hands at Beckhampton, Tree believed that Arc winner Rainbow Quest was the best. "Not only was he very good but he was genuine and consistent. It was bad luck that he was born in the same year as El Gran Senor or he might have done even better, but he's proving himself as a stallion and I enjoy that very much".

The horse remembered most fondly, however, from the Beckhampton hall of fame came as something of a surprise, "I suppose it would have to be Constans, who was a very good sprinter and went on for a very long time. He didn't win any top races but an awful lot of tip-top handicaps. He was one of Miss Sheriffe's, who was always a lucky owner for me". Perhaps Constans' most notable achievement was to win the Prix de Saint George three years in a row, a characteristic triumph for Tree, who was a pioneer of European pot-hunting

The familiar, dapper figure of Jeremy Tree was to be seen at the races right until the end of his life, "if it's local and there's something interesting running" and out on the gallops, although the veteran of thirty eight seasons admitted that "second lot is quite early enough for me these days".

Finally, I asked wether there was any feeling of regret at giving up training when, in the year after retirement, the winners of the French and English Derby were sent out from Beckhampton, particularly as Quest for Fame and Sanglamore had both been trained by Tree as two year olds?

The answer was typically generous: "I was quite simply delighted and there was no feeling of regret at all. It was much more important that Roger had set off well. Although I'd trained them both as two year olds, they weren't at all precocious. Roger did a brilliant job being so patient with them both"

The late Jeremy Tree,
Master of Beckhampton.

BECKHAMPTON, WILTSHIRE.

ROGER CHARLTON

BECKHAMPTON APPEARS AS a revelation to those who have never seen it. Far from the madding crowds of the Suffolk heaths, here is a veritable private Newmarket: five hundred acres of the finest rolling downland gallops anywhere, for the exclusive use of the incumbent trainer. The person lucky enough to enjoy the position at present is Roger Charlton, who became only the fifth trainer at Beckhampton in over a century when he succeeded Jeremy Tree in 1990.

Casting an eye over the wide open expanse of the Downs at Beckhampton, it is easy to see why the legendary Sam and Fred Darling carried all before them in the racing world of the first half of this century, winning no less than nine Derbys between them. During the war, when the vast majority of Britain's gallops were ploughed up for food production, the wide expanses of Beckhampton's summer gallops (Crown Property since time immemorial), where King George VI's Sun Chariot was prepared for the 1942 filly's Triple Crown, remained untouched.

And yet the yard's origins could hardly be more humble. Beckhampton House itself dates back to the mid-eighteenth century, when the keeper of the Catherine Wheel Inn at nearby Avebury built another Inn of the same name at the Beckhampton crossroads (now a busy roundabout). By the mid-nineteenth century it had become known as the Beckhampton House Inn and the incumbent, William Treene, had taken to training as a sideline.

Beckhampton trainer, Roger Charlton, accompanied by his vet, inspect a filly on the sick list.

It was not until 1880, however, when Sam Darling became the proprietor, that Beckhampton began to assume its place in turf folklore. Much of the yard dates from that period and bears the ordered, almost military stamp of the Darling persona. In traditional style, the neat quadrangle of the main yard is overseen by a large clock, reminding the staff of exactly where they should be at a given time in the yard's unchanging routine - particularly vital in the Darling era, where the authority of the trainer was absolute.

The lads' accommodation has been tagged onto the back of the house in what Mr Tree described as "Heath Robinson" style extensions. It is a close knit little community, now sadly diminished by the

Apart from the addition of a colour-coordinated flower bed (above) the trim stable yard at Beckhampton has changed little in over a hundred years.

death of the former trainer, who dearly loved to be surrounded by his former charges, who would always greet their former boss with a crisply delivered 'Sir', when they met him about the yard.

The objects of the lads' diurnal routines, the horses, are housed in what the former trainer calls "the best boxes you'll find anywhere": spacious, seasoned timber 'apartments', heavily reinforced with studding to absorb the impact of a kick. Cool in summer and cosy in winter, both Tree and Charlton swear by them, although the cost of maintaining their century old exteriors can be a headache. The common feeling is that it is one well worth enduring for what Charlton describes as "the privilege of training from an old historic yard".

That the boxes have lasted so long without bearing signs of wear is a testament to the Darlings' meticulous attention to detail. Nothing was too much trouble for the Beckhampton horses. In the 'New Yard' built across the road by Fred Darling in 1927, the stable was fitted with that state of the art invention, central heating (the old radiators still survive today). Unfortunately, in the first year of operation, virtually all the horses in that yard became ill and the newfangled machines were never switched on again.

Watching the orderly institution that is Beckhampton at the observances of its daily routine, one is reminded of a particularly well-disciplined public school, the apparently chaotic bustle of the strings coming and going periodically erupting like the switchover between lessons, the noise subsiding to a miraculous calm as the work of the morning finishes, a peace interrupted only by the horses chomping contentedly at their mangers.

Cool in summer and cosy in winter, Beckhampton's atmospheric old boxes have stood the test of time.

The horses at Beckhampton certainly seem more relaxed and contented than most. The 'Beckhampton Bloom' so often associated with the Darling horses in the past has been passed on. Jeremy Tree, who until his death lived on in the main house - part of the lads' hostel directly above his dining room - remembered the irritation he felt in his early days as a trainer, arriving at a local track like Bath with an unraced two year old to find it made "a raging favourite". "Inevitably, they would rate the Beckhampton horses highly and we almost couldn't help them looking well".

The contentment and relaxation of all Beckhampton's occupants - equine and human - is central to the philosophy of Mr Tree's successor, Roger Charlton, who believes that it contributes to the yard's success. "It's a tranquil place. You can go where you like, when you like". Unlike many yards, there are no roads to negotiate with skittish horses, before a morning's work can begin. The yard opens out straight onto the Downs, which stretch out uninterruptedly almost as far as the eye can see. For some people, such isolation could pose a problem in itself, a fact which Roger Charlton acknowledges. "Sometimes it can be a lonely place to train - there's nobody to compare notes with or work horses with - but you don't have to rush out at a given time and the horses do seem to respond to the relaxed atmosphere".

Beckhampton is a place that seems to inspire loyalty and continuity. The average length of service is unusually high in an industry characterised by the itinerance of its workforce. After sixteen years at Beckhampton, the 'new guv'nor' still maintains that compared with some of the Beckhampton staff, he is still a newcomer. Edgar Blake, the gallops man, predates Mr Tree (who arrived in 1953) and former head lad Dai Rees, who was apprenticed to Fred Darling, has not long retired.

Fred Darling trained seven Derby winners at Beckhampton betweem 1922 and 1941.

Roger Charlton, like Jeremy Tree before him, is very aware of the yard's history and traditions and, above all, clearly loves the place, but he is not one to bury his head in the downland turf and forget about harsh economic realities. The expense involved in maintaining Beckhampton's unrivalled facilities is considerable and a modern trainer cannot afford to stand still.

"If one just has thirty ordinary winners to one's credit in a place like this, the sums just do not add up. I'm very conscious of how the whole operation is financed. Out here in the wilds, we have twelve cottages to maintain and, in order to get the best, we pay the lads 25 per cent more than the average. Up until now we've been lucky and we've had a couple of good horses to keep the place going. In Mr Tree's day, we were sent 30 yearlings by Mr Abdulla, but now that figure is halved. The chances of finding that elusive horse have diminished".

It would be a tragedy for the landscape of British horse racing if, one day, a lack of patronage made the glorious Beckhampton gallops, in all their grandeur, unviable. An attenuated version of the great old place, reduced maybe to a few grass gallops surrounding the ubiquitous woodchips and equitracks, would be a sorry sight indeed.

PAST TRAINERS:
Sam and Fred Darling; Noel Murless; Gordon Richards; Jeremy Tree

PAST ASSISTANTS:
Bill Elsey: Roger Charlton

NOTABLE HORSES:
Ard Patrick; Galtee More; Sun Chariot; Coronach; Cameronian; Owen Tudor; Hurry On; Pasch; Big Game; Captain Cuttle; Pont L'Eveque; Manna; Tudor Minstrel; Abernant; Only For Life; Constans; Juliette Marny; Scintillate; Known Fact; Rainbow Quest; Sanglamore; Quest for Fame.

OWNERS:
K.Abdulla; Miss.M.Sheriffe; Lord Weinstock; Terry Ellis; J.Tree; The Earl of Derby; A.F.Budge (Equine) Ltd; Helena Springfield Ltd; Sir Philip Oppenheimer; A.N.C.Bengough; Christopher Heath; Jocelyn Hambro; S.S.Niarchos; Dr.C.Stelling; Mrs N.Myers; T.D.Rootes; Mrs A.Skiffington; M.Arnold; Michael Broke; Mrs Jayne Wrightsman; Exors of the late Mrs J.de.Rothschild; D.F.Chaplin; Mrs.J.Baker; J.G.Charlton;

WHATCOMBE, OXFORDSHIRE.

PAUL COLE

FOR SEVEN SEASONS between 1978 and 1985, the gallops at Woolley Down were silent. The famous turf, which had been graced so memorably by the likes of the 'Flying Mumty', Mumtaz Mahal, and the great Blandford, no longer echoed, as it had done for three quarters of a century, with the sound of thoroughbred hooves in strong work. The retirement of Arthur Budgett, who had trained so successfully at Whatcombe since 1951, left a vacuum, which his assistant, James Bethell, was unable to fill in the recession-hit climate of the late 1970s.

Unused the Whatcombe gallops may have been but, in the tight-knit racing community of the Berkshire Downs, they were in no danger of being forgotten. By the mid-1980s, the economic climate was once again looking up and Lambourn trainer, Paul Cole, was bursting at the seams of his Hill House yard and getting increasingly frustrated with the nightmare of organising a big string on the congested public gallops. From this perspective, the privacy and quality of the Whatcombe gallops held considerable appeal for Cole and his main owner, Prince Fahd Salman.

After seven years of laying empty, the yard at Whatcombe was not a pretty sight. "It was an absolute dump" according to Paul Cole, "it was a question of whether we would pull most of it down or whether it would fall down of its own accord". For Cole, the state of the yard was largely incidental. The gallops were the thing. "It is such fabulous turf here. If you are going to work valuable horses, the most crucial consideration is finding the right surface and at

Mrs Cole leads the string back home after second lot.

Whatcombe, the gallops must be among the top three in the country".

Third lot troop off down the long drive. In the distance is the winter cantering ground where the great Blandford broke down.

The Whatcombe gallops were first laid down at the end of the last century by an Irishman, Richard Cecil (Dick) Dawson, who took out a lease on the land in 1897 and proceeded to convert the farm from agriculture to racing. Like his friend and fellow Irishman, Atty Persse, Dawson (who was no relation of the famous Scottish training clan) was, initially at least, more interested in steeplechasing, with the consequence that, in its earliest years as a racing stable, Whatcombe produced more jumpers than flat race horses. The year after his arrival, Dawson sent out one of the horses he had brought from Ireland, Drogheda, to win the Grand National.

Flat racing thoroughbreds first began to appear at Whatcombe during the Edwardian era, when Dawson acquired the valuable patronage of Lord Carnarvon. From that moment on, the balance of the yard's intake was tilted towards the flat. In the years that followed, some of the most influential bloodlines in British racing would be channelled through Dick Dawson's highly successful training operation. Arguably the most important of these came about not through patronage but because of a fortuitous purchase at the sales. A yearling colt called Blandford, dismissed by many at the December sales of 1920 because he was too straight in front, was snapped up by Dawson for 720 guineas, in whose ownership he remained. Early the next year on Woolley Down, Blandford began to display a frustrating combination of brilliance and fragility on the gallops. Although he won the Princess of Wales Stakes at Newmarket before breaking down on the Far Sanfoin canter at Whatcombe, Blandford was never able to fulfill on the racecourse the exceptional promise he showed at home.

The Dawson stud, Cloghran in County Dublin, was to be Blandford's proving ground. Over the next two decades he proved himself the leading stallion of his generation, producing such horses as Blenheim, Windsor Lad, Bahram, Udaipur, Pasch and Trigo. A goodly number of his best offspring predictably found their way to Whatcombe, including the aforementioned Trigo, who won the Derby and St Leger in 1929. Blandford is buried in a grave behind the yard, fitting testimony to a horse who was the basis of so much of the yard's later success.

The other cornerstone of Whatcombe's racing history was the legendary 'Flying Mumty', Mumtaz Mahal, who arrived at Whatcombe as part of the second consignment of two year olds sent to Dawson by the Aga Khan, who quickly became Dawson's principal patron. Her exploits, both at home and on the racecourse have passed into racing folklore. As recently as 1992, when the performances of another flying filly, Lyric Fantasy, caught the eye, she was

Snurge relaxes in the freedom of a pen the day after racing.

immediately compared with her illustrious predecessor. At stud, too, Mumtaz Mahal's influence for speed has reverberated down the generations; although she herself produced no top class offspring, the talent seemed to skip a generation and her daughters produced a whole host of important horses, including Mahmoud, Star Of Iran and Nasrullah.

Dawson was a gentleman trainer and very much his own man. He objected to insinuations that he had not been trying with one of the Aga Khan's horses and ordered the Aga's entire string out of the yard at the end of the 1930 season, even though it reduced numbers at Whatcombe by half. He had been champion trainer three times during the time that the Aga Khan had been principal patron. After the departure of the Aga's horses to Frank Butters' Fitzroy House yard at Newmarket, Dawson never reached those heights again, although he continued training until 1945.

After a five year interregnum, during which time Michael Blackmore trained at the yard, the classic tradition at Whatcombe was maintained by Arthur Budgett, who trained two Derby winners, in Blakeney and Morston, during his 24 seasons at the helm. He was also champion trainer in 1969, the year of Blakeney's Derby.

Reviving such a potent tradition was a mouthwatering prospect for someone as steeped in racing history as Paul Cole. Together with his partner and principal patron, Prince Fahd Salman, Cole bought the yard in 1985. "It was a unique opportunity. I could have bought it myself and spent ten years doing it up as and when I could afford to or, I could buy it with a partner and do it up to Grade One standard in one go. It was extremely exciting to be able to redesign the place, exactly how I wanted it".

Whatcombe today has a thoroughly updated and expanded yard to match its superlative gallops. Arthur Budgett's main yard survives but is now flanked, symmetrically, by a new yard, doubling the previous capacity. Over 130 horses can now be trained at the yard. An indoor school, swimming pool and all weather gallops ensure that they do so in some style.

It is the Whatcombe gallops that really cause Paul Cole to enthuse. "They are the essence of the place" says the Master of Whatcombe. "In summer, we use Woolley Down, which has the best or, at least, equal best, turf in the world, in my opinion, and then there is the winter gallop at Summerdown, which is only used when the ground is soft and does not cut up". In addition to these, there is the picturesque cantering ground on the hill facing the yard, known as Far Sanfoin (famous as the place where Blandford broke down) and the new 'Paradise' all weather gallops directly above the yard.

Thanks to Paul Cole and Prince Fahd, Whatcombe is now once again a force to be reckoned with in racing circles. At the end of the 1991 season - the year of Generous' triumphs - with

Head lad Colin Ratcliffe, who has been with Paul Cole for almost twenty years.

prize money totalling over £125 million, Paul Cole followed in the footsteps of Dick Dawson and Arthur Budgett and became the third Whatcombe trainer to achieve the status of champion trainer. The yard had, at long last, re-assumed its rightful place as one of the top training establishments in the country.

PAST TRAINERS:
*Mr McNaughton; Dick Dawson; Michael Blackmore;
Arthur Budgett; James Bethell*

PAST ASSISTANTS:
Penn Curzon-Howe; Jonathan Powell; Michael Bell

NOTABLE HORSES:
*Drogheda; Blandford; Mumtaz Mahal; Diophon; Salmon Trout; Trigo; Brownhylda;
Zucchero; Derring Do; Huntercombe; Petty Officer; Blakeney; Morston; Dominion;
Ibn Bey; Snurge; Zoman; Generous; Ruby Tiger; Dilum*

OWNERS:
*Prince Fahd Salman; Prince Faisal; Sheikh Mohammed;
HRH Sultan Ahmed Shah; Viscountess Portman; Athos Christodoulou;
Christopher Wright; Richard Green;
Sir George Meyrick; M. Arbib; J.S. Gutkin;
Yahya Nasib; Philip Blacker;
Lord Donoughmore; Mrs Jane Lewis*

BEDFORD HOUSE, NEWMARKET.

LUCA CUMANI

BEARING THE TITLE, 'Master of Bedford House', is the sort of English racing tradition that still makes Luca Cumani smile, even after seventeen years of occupying the position. The independent training empires of Newmarket, and particularly the historic surroundings of Bedford House, are far removed from the shared racecourse stables of San Siro, in which the young would-be trainer might have begun his career had he not first tasted the fruits of training on Newmarket Heath.

"When I first came to Newmarket, I was overwhelmed by it. Newmarket itself might not be the most beautiful town and the landscape is not the best England has to offer but from the point of view of a would-be trainer, 3,000 acres of well cared for gallops and the chance to be boss of one's own yard with enough space to carry on the business of training, was very inviting".

Bedford Cottage, the old trainers' house, with Victorian trainer, Jimmy Jewitt, on the left .

"I used to come past the gates of Bedford House down the Bury Road, when I was with Henry Cecil. I peered in and saw that the house was attractive. When I started looking for a place to train, it had been on the market, vacant, for about eighteen months, since the death of Jack Clayton".

The young trainer took advantage of the slump in property prices and bought Bedford House for the bargain price of £75,000. It had cost Jack Clayton, the previous owner, £15,000 in 1929! Until Luca Cumani purchased the yard and began the process of transforming it into one of Newmarket's 'big four' public stables (along with its near neighbours on the Bury Road, Stanley House and Freemason Lodge, and of course, the pre-eminent Warren Place), Bedford House, formerly known as Bedford Cottage, had always been essentially a private stable, owned and managed closely by a racing type now largely extinct. Neither trainer nor sole owner, these men of the turf employed resident trainers for the day-to-day business of training, but closely superintended the operation themselves.

In its 130 year history, Bedford Cottage/House has been associated with three such racing characters: Captain James Machell, the fearless gambler who managed and gambled on other people's horses as well as his own, the vastly wealthy Colonel Harry McCalmont who was a

The ivy-clad flint buildings of the main yard at Bedford House are among the most attractive at 'Headquarters'.

more conventional patron and, latterly, Jack Clayton, who employed a number of trainers during the course of his long career.

Bedford Cottage, as it was originally known, was a model training establishment of its day. It was a solidly built yard, flint walled for coolness in summer and warmth in winter, with its own fresh water supply drawn from a well and fed from a crenellated water tower of a height to match its pretension. Significantly, there was also a trainer's house of some size and gentility in addition to a number of small cottages for the upper echelons of the stable staff. Under a late nineteenth century illustration of Bedford Cottage in the *Racing Illustrated* magazine of June 23rd 1893, is the following caption: "The homes of trainers of the present day afford a curious contrast to the dwellings of most of their old time predecessors, who were content to pass much of their life in houses of primitive fashion and marked by few attempts at outside ornament. The reverse is now customary and the dwellings of many of our trainers - Mr Jewitt amongst the number - are tasteful and neat to a high degree".

Although, since its inception in the 1860s, Bedford House has been recognised as one of the leading yards in Newmarket, its capacity in 1976 was still only 45 boxes, sufficient to make it a leading contender for honours in the nineteenth century but, in the era of mega 100 box plus yards, only big enough for the second division. In Luca Cumani's early days at Bedford House the confines of the old yard did not prove onerous. Like many of the trainers now training huge strings at Newmarket, Cumani's expansion as a trainer has been gradual. "You have to prove that you can manage well with 60, 80 and 100 horses before people will entrust you with more".

Rather than alter the original yard or move, Cumani's response to the space problem at Bedford House was to build new barns as the need arose on the site of an old orchard between the existing yard and the paddocks. "We built one when Sheikh Mohammed arrived and another when the Aga Khan came". These small "nucleii", as the ever-erudite Cumani refers to them, are treated almost as independent entities within the yard. Each of these twenty-stall barns has a head lad responsible for its administration.

The next major expansion was to lease the land adjacent to Bedford House and occupy the forty-box yard known as the Kremlin. This meant that the total capacity for both yards had grown to 150, making it one of the largest training establishments on one site in Newmarket. There is a tremendous sense of space about the newly expanded Bedford House that is quite unlike the almost claustrophobic atmosphere one occasionally senses in some of the town's yards. Even with fifty horses circling round in one of the massive lots that are a feature of the modern Newmarket, there is enough green space all around for it to feel like the open country.

The yard's best-known landmark, its crenellated water tower.

Despite the large number of horses in his care, Luca Cumani believes that the level of individual attention that each horse receives does not suffer. "I see them all every morning at exercise, of course, and then at the end of each morning I tour round with each of the head lads and then again at evening stables, so each one of their names goes through my head at least three times a day, so there is no doubt that they are all known individually and intimately. In fact, provided you are well organised I believe it is a positive advantage to train a large number because it is easier to arrange the gallops in appropriate groups. You can then become much more accurate in forecasting the abilities of the various horses by working them together. I think this is one of the reasons why the top level of trainers have such relatively high strike rates".

As luck would have it, just as the yard reached the peak of its operating potential, Bedford House was hit by the double whammy of the recession and the departure from British racing of Cumani's principal patron, the Aga Khan. "Three years ago I had thought I was in a good position, almost invulnerable in fact, because I had a good spread of well-established owners but it just goes to show that one can never predict the future".

Bearing in mind the loss of the Aga Khan's horses and the effects of the recession, Luca Cumani appears to be weathering the storm comparatively well. There are still at least one hundred horses in the yard and he is not unduly reliant on any one owner. "I think a trainer operates best with the least pressure and I think a one owner situation would inevitably put pressure on the trainer".

Typically, Luca Cumani is already looking beyond the immediate problems of the recession to the possible dangers of the next boom. "The only difficulty I foresee for Newmarket in the future is that with the development of the Hamilton Road and the expansion in the number of yards, the inevitable consequence is that when we come out of recession there will be far too many horses in Newmarket, which will create considerable traffic problems for the horses and an inevitable deterioration of the gallops".

Master and Mistress of Bedford House, Luca and Sara Cumani.

Training racehorses is something Luca Cumani sees in a broader context. "Trainers are professionals. An owner should approach a trainer in the same way that he would go to an accountant, and put himself in their hands". Luca Cumani is one of the few trainers that really inspires such confidence and fully deserves the appellation of professional trainer.

PAST TRAINERS:

Norman Bertie; J. Cannon; Noel Cannon; Charles and George Bloss; Jimmy Jewitt; Major Charles Beatty; Major Jack Clayton.

NOTABLE HORSES:

Hermit; Isinglass; Zinfandel; Pinza; Belle of All; Three Legs; Old Country; Tolomeo; Commanche Run; Kahyasi; Then Again; Second Set; Shamshir.

OWNERS:

Sheikh Mohammed; Sheikh Ahmed Al Maktoum; Prince Sultan Mohammed; Richard Duchossois; Gerald Leigh; Lord Hartington; Edward P. Evans; Lord White of Hull; Baron Edouard de Rothschild; Robert P. Levy; Osvaldo Pedroni; W.S. Farish III; L. Del Balzo Di Presenzano.

Castle Stables, Arundel.

John Dunlop

The picturesque surroundings of the park at Arundel provide what appears to be the perfect backdrop for the training of racehorses. Unsurprisingly, after almost three decades at such a grindstone, John Dunlop gives the impression of a man content with his appointed lot. Only the cigarette constantly to hand and a certain air of distraction give any clue to the pressures that accompany training at the highest level.

Watching the fifty-strong second lot taking a turn in the shade of some beech trees, racehorses seem a well-established fixture of Arundel's pastoral scene. In fact, they are only a relatively recent addition. Although the odd horse has been trained on the downs at various times in the past two or three hundred years, the present gallops were laid down during the latter part of the Second World War.

John Dunlop in discussion with assistant trainer, Robert Alcock.

Before the war, Bernard, the then Duke of Norfolk and his wife Lavinia, had horses with Victor Gilpin, initially at Newmarket but then at Michelgrove, near Findon on the South Downs, which formed part of the Duke's estate. At the outbreak of the war, Gilpin joined the army and the gallops at Michelgrove were requisitioned for the war effort and rendered virtually useless by the wear and tear of heavy machinery.

It was at this juncture that the Duke decided to bring the horses across the downs to Arundel. Although there was reasonably extensive stabling at the Castle for carriage horses, there was nothing like enough room for a large string of racehorses and no facilities whatsoever for exercising them, apart from a very large deer park full of mature trees.

With Herculean effort and singlemindedness, the Duke and Duchess set about organising a programme of tree felling and ground levelling. Within two years, the present gallops had been created and the services of William Smyth, one of five members of that great racing dynasty then training, secured as the family's private trainer. The problem of accommodation was solved at one fell swoop with the transportation, lock, stock and barrel, of the old wooden

Taking a turn in the main yard. The wooden boxes were transported by the previous Duke of Norfolk from another yard.

boxes from Michelgrove, which were placed neatly in the middle of the main yard at Castle Stables, where they remain to this day.

Remarkably, when William Smyth embarked on his first season at Arundel (with Lavinia, Duchess of Norfolk seeing to the entries and organising the paper work) he had 46 horses in his charge, one of the largest strings in the country at the time. Sadly, the Duke's and Duchess" enthusiasm was not repaid with racecourse success and the really good horses eluded them. Ironically, Arundel's best horse of that era, Skymaster, who won the Middle Park, arrived in 1960, the year of William Smyth's retirement. He was succeeded by his son, Gordon Smyth, who trained at Arundel until 1965, when he took over from "Towser" Gosden at Heath House, Lewes (winning the Derby in his first year with Charlottown).

This left his twenty seven year old assistant, John Dunlop, in charge. It was a rare opportunity for a young man without racing connections and a daunting prospect for someone with only four years racing experience, two of these having been spent at Neville Dent's small National Hunt yard. "I was very lucky. At the time, there were very few young men training. Most trainers were ex-jockeys or from racing families and there wasn't the pattern of apprenticeship to top trainers that has now been established". The experience of assisting Neville Dent proved invaluable to Dunlop. "Nowadays in a big yard, there is a clearly defined hierarchy and an assistant might not get to deviate from his narrow area of responsibility, whereas in a small National Hunt yard at that time, I found myself doing anything and everything and learned a great deal in a very short time".

Training at Arundel is not as easy as it looks. The estate lies right at the southern tip of the South Downs and, unlike racing's Berkshire heartland, it is not true downland, in that the ground is not entirely "on the chalk" but a mixture of chalk and clay, with the consequence that the ground is often too soft to use in the spring and too dry at the height of the summer.

Alhaajib, a half brother to Lahib, looks on while the rest of the string take a pick of grass in the park.

Understandably Dunlop professes himself to be "very dependent on all weather surfaces" and was one of the first major trainers in the country to experiment with them. In addition to the main grass gallops at Arundel, which rise in a series of parallel exercise strips up quite a stiff climb, there is a five and a half furlong woodchip running alongside, which is used for everyday cantering, a sand canter and the main all weather gallop, which is twelve furlongs round with room for three upsides. It is mostly uphill, so "they don't have to go very fast to achieve the same work rate as they would on a flat heath".

The storm of 1987 decimated the Arundel landscape, removing whole swathes of trees from the horizon. Dunlop was in Newmarket at the time of the storm and returned home to find a scene of utter devastation. However, Castle Stables' long-serving trainer has done his best to repair the damage. Although only a tenant, Dunlop looks after the landscape as though it is his own, planting new trees to replace those lost in the storm, and taking a keen interest in their development.

Valentine, the guvnor's hack is distinguished in his own right: sixth in the Horse of the Year Show.

At the beginning, like William and Gordon Smyth before him, Dunlop was a paid employee, training exclusively for the Duke and his family and their immediate circle of friends. For the old Duke, the training of racehorses, like the first class cricket played on the estate's cricket ground in the Park, was a private passion indulged on a grand scale. It is now very much a cost-effective business.

For many years now, Dunlop has been a public trainer with all that entails, coping diplomatically with the vicissitudes involved in looking after a large number of owners as well as horses. The pressure has been eased considerably by the advent of Arab involvement in British horse racing - Dunlop was the Maktoum family's first trainer in this country in the late 1970s - but Dunlop has always sought to develop and maintain a broad-based patronage. In the present economic climate, this has not been easy. "These are difficult times for the racehorse owning classes. The day of the big owner-breeders has largely passed and quite apart from the recession, the huge capital losses suffered by the names at Lloyds - just the sort of people to have an interest in a horse - has had quite an effect".

John Dunlop sorts out the morning's exercise in the shade of some beech trees.

Thankfully, the Maktoum connection remains as strong as ever. The stream that brought such quality horses as Salsabil and Shadayid to the yard continues to flow. At the time of writing, that superb looking son of Riverman, Lahib, had just won the Queen Elizabeth II Stakes at the Festival of British Racing and was soon to be joined in the yard by a full brother to Salsabil, freshly purchased at the Goffs Orby sale by Sheikh Hamdan.

It is clear why someone like Sheikh Hamdan should choose to send horses to Arundel. Anyone who has heard Dunlop talk about the variety of animals in his care, whether they be prize cattle, show horses or racehorses, knows that he is passionate about animal husbandry and a true connoisseur of the beau ideal.

PAST TRAINERS:
W.A. Smyth; Gordon Smyth

NOTABLE HORSES:
Skymaster; Scottish Rifle; Ragstone; Shirley Heights; Quick as Lightning; Circus Plume; Moon Madness; Salsabil; Shadayid; Lahib.

OWNERS:
Sheikh Hamdan Al Maktoum; Prince Faisal; Duke of Marlborough; Lord Halifax; Lord Chelsea; Lady Cohen; Sir Robin McAlpine; Lord and Lady Swaythling; D.R. Hunnisett; P.G. Goulandris; David Sieff; Gerencon Italia; Miss Peggy Kwoh; Mrs Roger Waters; Frank Stronach; S. Khaled; Miss K. Rausing; Cyril Humphris; Aubrey Ison; Sir Gordon Reece; Miss B. Swire; Sir Thomas Pilkington; Windflower Overseas Holdings Ltd; Anthony Pye-Jeary; Tom Wilson; E. Penser; Vijay Mallya; Colin Southgate.

HIGHFIELD HOUSE, MALTON.

BILL ELSEY

N ITS PRIME, Highfield House bore comparison with any training establishment in the country. For the best part of a century, it had been one of the great powerhouses of northern racing, its equine inhabitants regular contenders for classic honours and the three families associated with the estate, Scott, I'Anson and Elsey, were turf institutions.

Horses were first trained at Highfield as early as the eighteenth century, long before any of the current buildings on the site were erected. The first recorded trainer was George Searle, who began training at Highfield in 1780 while still a jockey and rode the winner of the St Leger three times in the next ten years. The next notable trainer at Highfield was the intemperate Will Scott, a tough, hard drinking jockey who was the younger brother of the legendary trainer, John Scott of Whitewall, for whom he rode 14 classic winners. William Scott married well and had enough money to set himself up at Highfield, where he installed William Oates as trainer, while supervising operations and riding the

Bill Elsey in front of Highfield House.

The same view a century earlier, soon after the house's construction.

horses himself. In 1846, he narrowly missed becoming the first owner/rider of a Triple Crown winner, when Sir Tatton Sykes, a horse he had bought for £100 from a local farmer, failed to follow up his success in the Derby with a win in the St Leger because of his own drunkenness in the saddle.

In 1863, the estate was sold to William I'Anson, who trained a number of classic winners, most notably Blink Bonny and Blair Athol, from the nearby Spring Cottage stables. By the time of I'Anson's death in 1881, he had become one of the largest property owners in the area, so that his eldest son, also called William, inherited considerable wealth and local influence, as well as a famous racing name. Another son, Miles, inherited the family home and the Blink Bonny Stud, but it was William, who kept the racing name alive and developed Highfield House into one of the most impressive training establishments in Malton, with private gallops rivalling the public gallops at Langton Wold. In addition, he built a short-lived steeplechase and hurdle race course immediately adjacent to the stables. The racecourse, known as Malton races, was closed down on the insistence of the then principal stable patron, Charles Perkins, who wanted the course to be used exclusively as a training ground.

William I'Anson's string on the Highfield gallops.

Highfield House itself was not built until some years after I'Anson moved back for good (the rather meanly appointed cottage that formerly served as the trainer's house was one of young William's main reasons for a brief and unsuccesful sojourn at Hambleton House), and is a monument to Victorian self-confidence in general and to the local importance of the I'Anson dynasty in particular. It is very much a purpose-built racing house, complete with a stained glass triptych above the stair–well recalling the family's racing successes with depictions of Blink Bonny and Blair Athol, accompanying a portrait of Fred Archer.

Despite having some notable successes in a long career, William I'Anson Junior never matched the achievements of his father. In his training methods, he was something of an anachronism, persisting with the by then outmoded habits of sweating and bleeding horses, to reduce 'grossness' and thin the blood respectively. In 1908, almost forty years after he began his career at Highfield House, I'Anson let the stable and surrounding land to Sir John Thursby, who installed F.C. Archer, a nephew of the great Fred Archer, as his private trainer. In conjunction with I'Anson, Sir John built an imposing new yard half a mile from the old Highfield House, complete with 'a covered-in exercise yard and riding school'.

The partnership was interrupted by the First World War, after which Highfield, along with the Blink Bonny Stud, were sold by I'Anson to a wealthy Lancastrian turfite called C.F. Kenyon, for £30,000. Kenyon, who raced under the assumed name of Mr.K. Tilstock, expanded the operation considerably and with his private trainer, H.D. Bazley, controlled a large string from the yard before his death in 1924. Without Kenyon's patronage, Bazley could not continue at Highfield, which was eventually sold to a man who would finally establish the yard as one of the great powerhouses of British racing.

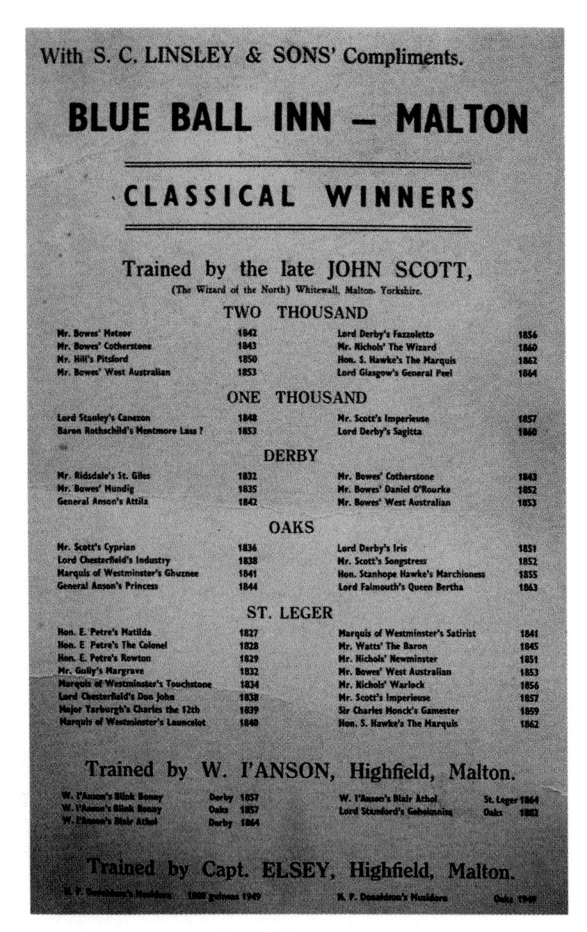

With S. C. LINSLEY & SONS' Compliments.

BLUE BALL INN – MALTON

CLASSICAL WINNERS

Trained by the late JOHN SCOTT,

(The Wizard of the North) Whitewall, Malton. Yorkshire.

TWO THOUSAND

Mr. Bowes' Meteor	1842	Lord Derby's Fazzoletto	1856
Mr. Bowes' Cotherstone	1843	Mr. Nichols' The Wizard	1860
Mr. Hill's Pitsford	1850	Hon. S. Hawke's The Marquis	1862
Mr. Bowes' West Australian	1853	Lord Glasgow's General Peel	1864

ONE THOUSAND

Lord Stanley's Canezon	1848	Mr. Scott's Imperieuse	1857
Baron Rothschild's Mentmore Lass ?	1853	Lord Derby's Sagitta	1860

DERBY

Mr. Ridsdale's St. Giles	1832	Mr. Bowes' Cotherstone	1843
Mr. Bowes' Mundig	1835	Mr. Bowes' Daniel O'Rourke	1852
General Anson's Attila	1842	Mr. Bowes' West Australian	1853

OAKS

Mr. Scott's Cyprian	1836	Lord Derby's Iris	1851
Lord Chesterfield's Industry	1838	Mr. Scott's Songstress	1852
Marquis of Westminster's Ghuznee	1841	Hon. Stanhope Hawke's Marchioness	1855
General Anson's Princess	1844	Lord Falmouth's Queen Bertha	1863

ST. LEGER

Hon. E. Petre's Matilda	1827	Marquis of Westminster's Satirist	1841
Hon. E Petre's The Colonel	1828	Mr. Watts' The Baron	1845
Hon. E. Petre's Rowton	1829	Mr. Nichols' Newminster	1851
Mr. Gully's Margrave	1832	Mr. Bowes' West Australian	1853
Marquis of Westminster's Touchstone	1834	Mr. Nichols' Warlock	1856
Lord Chesterfield's Don John	1838	Mr. Scott's Imperieuse	1857
Major Yarburgh's Charles the 12th	1839	Sir Charles Monck's Gamester	1859
Marquis of Westminster's Launcelot	1840	Hon. S. Hawke's The Marquis	1862

Trained by W. I'ANSON, Highfield, Malton.

W. I'Anson's Blink Bonny	Derby	1857	W. I'Anson's Blair Athol	St. Leger	1864
W. I'Anson's Blink Bonny	Oaks	1857	Lord Stamford's Geheimniss	Oaks	1882
W. I'Anson's Blair Athol	Derby	1864			

Trained by Capt. ELSEY, Highfield, Malton.

N. P. Donaldson's Musidora	1000 guineas	1949	N. P. Donaldson's Musidora	Oaks	1949

A tally of Malton's classic winners.

Captain C.F. Elsey was a second generation trainer, his father having carved quite a reputation from his farm at Baumber in Lincolnshire, where he trained one of the largest strings of the late Victorian and Edwardian era. After a brief beginning at Glasgow House, Middleham, the young Charles Elsey's attempt to follow in his father's footsteps was interrupted by the First World War, in which he served with distinction, winning a Military Cross.

After the war, Captain Elsey was warned against resuming a career in racing because it seemed a more than usually risky prospect in such an uncertain world, but the young war hero soon tired of an alternative career as a farmer and began training in Scotland, at Clyde House, Ayr in 1921. After some important early successes, including the top local race, the Ayr Gold Cup, the death of his father in 1922 enabled Captain Elsey to gather together enough capital to buy Highfield.

Within a few years he had attracted an impressive retinue of owners, including the once all-conquering Duke of Portland, and achieved some notable successes in big northern races like the Northumberland Plate, with the result that the stabling had to be extended considerably. The new yard, Highfield, became used as the main yard, with Highfield House used as an overspill.

In Captain Elsey's heyday, between 1948 and 1960, during which time the yard sent out six classic winners and was rarely out of the top six in the trainers' table, the domination of Newmarket as a training centre was not so pronounced and northern trainers were able to compete on more equal terms with their southern counterparts.

Highfield's gradual decline in recent years has mirrored the relentless ebbing of the north's racing fortunes. Captain Elsey's son Bill, who took over from his father in 1961, has faced an uphill struggle ever since to maintain the scale of the operation at Highfield, which had expanded into one of the largest training establishments in the country.

The recent sale of what had always been the main yard at Highfield in Captain Elsey's era, cut its capacity as a racing stable in half, although the gallops were retained. The now veteran Bill Elsey continues, valiantly, to fly the flag, doing remarkably well with the limited raw material at his disposal. "I'll probably die here", he says, with a wry smile.

Understandably, Bill Elsey has strong views about racing's finances and the north/south divide. "The decline that has gradually been creeping up on us has reflected the value of the prize money going downwards. It has become more and more difficult for owners and friends to justify having horses. When we started in 1961, the minimum prize was £207. If you won three races, you'd paid your training costs for the year. If this was still the case, I'm sure some of our old owners would be only too keen to have horses again".

The last Elsey star: Linpac West.

Looking at the superb expanse of gallops at Highfield, and taking into account the experience and proven ability of its dual classic-winning proprietor and the sheer convenience of racing in North Yorkshire, where there are six flat race tracks within a 50 mile radius, it is a sad sign of the times that potential owners are not clamouring at the door. Add to that, the relatively low cost of having a horse in training at Malton, which is considerably lower than Newmarket rates at around £140-50 per week, and the situation becomes an indictment of the shortsightedness of owners with horses at 'Headquarters'.

"I can't understand why we're not appreciated more up here, but I'm afraid it has been like that for a long time. The season after Pia won the Oaks, I only attracted one new owner and that was a man, whose doctor told him it would be therapeutic! And when Peleid won the Leger, all the pundits said it must have been a substandard race. You can't win".

Even in its reduced state, Bill Elsey's Highfield House stable is still a very impressive place: a historic racing house and a well planted estate graced by 250 acres of the finest gallops you could hope to find anywhere, including an all weather gallop and a peat moss strip. By comparison, the former main yard at Highfield is a forlorn sight and eloquent testament to the economic downturn in racing: on a hot morning in midsummer, when, in years gone by the yard would have hummed with activity, the clocktower, that metronome of a well-run yard, reads two 'o'clock and the quiet in the covered rides and empty boxes, is palpable. Its future, however, seems brighter: James Hetherton, the son of one of Bill Elsey's longstanding owners, intends to renew his licence for the forthcoming season but Bill himself has announced his retirement at the end of the 1993 season.

PAST TRAINERS:

George Searle; Tommy Sykes; William Scott; Charles Lund; William I'Anson Junior; F.C. Archer; H.D. Bazley; Captain C.F. Elsey.

NOTABLE HORSES:

Imperatrix; Sir Tatton Sykes; Jenny Howlett; Musidora; Nearula; Frieze; Honeylight; Cantelo; Pia; Peleid; Henry the Seventh; Don; Linpac West.

Owners:

Linpac Group Ltd; Avril Stanhope; Mrs M.C. Butler; A.J. Massingberd-Mundy; N. Hetherton; Herbert Green; T.W.G. Torrance

GLASGOW HOUSE, MIDDLEHAM.

TOMMY FAIRHURST

TOMMY 'SQUEAK' FAIRHURST and his close-knit family team have breathed new life into the historic Glasgow House yard in Middleham, restoring it to something like its former glory. By modern standards, it is only a small stable, with thirty or so boxes crammed into every nook and cranny of its venerable coursed rubble stone walls, but in the very different racing scene of the early nineteenth century, it was one of the great powerhouses of British training.

The stable became known as Glasgow House because of its association with the one of the 'characters' of the Victorian turf, the mercurial Lord Glasgow, notorious for his impatience with trainers, jockeys and horses (the latter were often summarily shot for not reaching the required standard). He was the principal patron for many years in the mid-nineteenth century, but the zenith of the yard's career came in 1822, when the then trainer, James Croft sent out the first four horses in the St Leger, an incredible feat elegantly commemorated in a contemporary stone plaque on the wall of the trainer's house.

Tommy Fairhurst.

Glasgow House stands right in the centre of this famous North Yorkshire racing town on the picturesquely named Swine Market, in the shadow of its best known landmark, the ruined castle. In the early morning, it is horses rather than swine that outnumber cars, as the various strings make their undulating way up the dry stone wall-lined road, past the Dante Stud, to the public training grounds on the Low and High Moors. Middleham is enjoying something of a revival in its fortunes these days, with the success of relative newcomers, such as Mark Johnston and Patrick Haslam, but in its heyday (which, as with Glasgow House, was the early nineteenth century) Middleham was pre-eminent as a training centre, particularly with regard to the important northern meetings at Doncaster and York.

Tommmy Fairhurst's recollection of Middleham's past might not be quite that extensive but it is longer and more vivid than most. He first arrived at Middleham from County Durham in 1942, when he was apprenticed to Matt Peacock's then all-conquering Manor House yard. It was a hard school and the 'guv'nor' was a hard taskmaster. Working for the princely sum of a

Glasgow House might not be the largest stable in Middleham, but it is one of the oldest and thanks to the efforts of the Fairhurst family, one of the best kept.

shilling a week, the lads slept three to a bed and were expected to assist with farm chores whenever stable duties allowed. "We worked twelve hours a day and were allowed only one week off a year, usually at Christmas. We were each given two rabbits and the exact train fare back to our home towns". Such was the exploitation of lads in those early days that when Tommy left to join the army, he was shocked to find that army pay was twenty times greater than his wages as a lad. "I felt like a king on twenty one shillings a week".

Despite the harshness of the life, there were compensations, not the least of which was the opportunity to sit on perhaps the greatest horse that Middleham has produced this century, Dante. "I never rode work on him but I was allowed to sit on him, walking, when Willie (Nevett) had finished for the day". Such was the horse's brilliance that, in his preparation for the Derby, Fairhurst recalls that "nothing could stay with him long enough to give him a proper workout, so they used to position three five-furlong sprinters at intervals around the High Moor and jump them off just before he reached them. He would still beat all of them".

The excitement of being involved with such an exceptionally brilliant horse made up for all the many privations and was sufficient to ensure that on finishing his National Service, try as he might to give up working with horses and seek better paid employment, the lure of racing was always too much.

Apart from spells showjumping in County Durham and an exciting period working in Malton with Jack Pearce's gambling stable (suffice to say Alex Bird was the principal owner) Tommy and his wife and right-hand woman, Margaret, have been at Middleham ever since, as a jockey and then trainer. Spells with Dick Colven at Glasgow House and a long and fruitful association with Jack Fawcus at Ashgill, up beyond the town between the High and Low Moors, led eventually to the Fairhurst's first venture into training, at neighbouring Tupgill, which they rented.

The Fairhursts' intention had always been to own their own yard, however, and as Tommy and Margaret don't believe in borrowing, it took several years of careful saving and

Pulling out into the streets of Middleham.

accumulating before they were able to realise their ambition. It must have been a very special moment for Tommy Fairhurst, when Glasgow House came on the market, to be able to pay outright for the yard where he had once been a struggling would-be jockey.

When the Fairhursts arrived at Glasgow House, it was far from being the home of their dreams and was in serious need of a complete overhaul. The haylofts and tack rooms were virtually unusable because of rotten floors and it proved impossible to turn a modern wagon around in the main yard, which had been built long before the internal combustion engine. After months of careful and painstaking renovation work, the yard was completed to Tommy and Margaret's satisfaction. Fifteen years on, the yard still looks as pretty as a picture and so full of period charm that it is hard to believe that its charming coursed rubble stone walls have been touched since the day the house was built two hundred years before.

From the elegant gate piers at the entrance to the rococo-style enamel clock bedded in pebbles that graces the arch to the back yard, Glasgow House is full of quality, as befits its status as a listed building. Unlike many racing people, Tommy and Margaret have broad interests outside the game - they are both avid antique collectors - and fully appreciate the yard's historic qualities.

The happy family-orientated ship at Glasgow House is a testament to the virtues of hard work and living within your means. You won't hear any bleating here about the recession and high overheads. Tommy's ex-jump jockey sons, Chris and Tony perform the duties of assistant trainer and head lad respectively. Chris' wife Judy regularly rides out, while wife Margaret does a sterling job organising the house and dealing with owners, press and anybody else who happens to stray into the yard with traditional Yorkshire hospitality and charm. Chris is being groomed to take over the licence from his father in the near future, although it is highly doubtful that Tommy will disappear from the scene altogether.

PAST TRAINERS:
James Croft; Tom Dawson; Captain C.F. Elsey;
Dick Colven; Peter Chisman.

NOTABLE HORSES:
Theodore; General Peel; Woodsome; Barry's Gamble.

OWNERS:
C.H Newton; Jimmy Turney; C.D.Barber Lomax; Laurel Racing;
G. Stephenson; Mrs D. Kain; David Bramley; P.J. Garthwaite;
Deeside Nurseries Ltd; George H. Leggott; M.J. Rozenbroek;
John Jackson; Mrs M. Morley; Miss M. Johnstone; Brian Cann;
W.E. Blenkinsop; Mrs V. Paxton;
B. Harland; B. Brownsword

Stanley House, Newmarket.

John Gosden

If the Houyhnhnms ever returned Gulliver's visit and made a small detour to Newmarket's Stanley House Stables, they would probably feel very much at home. Even horses endowed with superhuman reason and accustomed to standing on their hind legs and eating at high table would have difficulty finding fault with the standard of accommodation.

Stanley House is a place of captivating beauty, prestige and tradition, founded on the great wealth of the British landed gentry at its Edwardian peak and maintained today by the equally lavish patronage of the leading owner/breeder in contemporary British racing, Sheikh Mohammed Al-Maktoum. The story of Stanley House begins in 1893, when the eponymous Hon.F.A.Stanley became the 16th Earl of Derby, inheriting a vast fortune in the process. The new Lord Derby's first avowed intent was to see the famous family colours, 'black, white cap', carried once more with distinction on the racecourse. He appointed the former steeplechase jockey and fifth son of the Earl of Durham, the Honourable George Lambton, as his trainer and set him up at the Bedford Lodge stable in Newmarket, a few hundred yards down the Bury Road from the site of what would become Stanley House.

It was an auspicious beginning, helped by the misfortune of a near neighbour. One of the first horses the new Lord Derby bought, in 1894, was the yearling filly, Canterbury Pilgrim, purchased at the dispersal sale of the Duchess of Montrose's Sefton Stud, which was situated next door to Bedford Lodge. The filly went on to win the Oaks and become a considerable asset at stud, but it was the subsequent purchase of the land on which the Sefton Stud stood, which laid the foundation for what was to become the finest stable of its day.

George Lambton.

The purchase was prompted by a prolonged bout of what contemporary trainers refer to as 'the virus', as George Lambton recalls in his famous memoirs, *Men and Horses I have Known*: "For three years in succession: 1901; 1902 and 1903 we had an epidemic of what was called Newmarket Fever at the Bedford Lodge Stables and Lord Derby decided to buy the Sefton Stud Farm from the Duke of Montrose and build the Stanley House Stables. They were finished in 1903, but our ill luck pursued us there". This ill luck took many forms: a bout of 'pink eye' was followed in 1908 by a devastating fire, which Lambton discovered on his return from the races. Mercifully, although the damage was extensive, none of the horses was seriously injured. In a more built-up area of the town, the outcome could have been much worse but, as Lambton remembers, "most of the horses when free galloped round a circular track which I have at the back of the stables".

For the next three decades, the elegant figure of George Lambton, the prototype 'gentleman trainer', presided over Stanley House, winning over a dozen classics. Despite winning the Derby with Hyperion in his final season at Stanley House, Lambton was considered by the then Lord Derby to be too old, at the age of 73, to bear the responsibility of training a large string. In fact, Lambton, already the doyen of his profession, continued training for another twelve years, retiring only two days before his death, at the age of eighty five in 1945.

Stanley House Stables remained essentially a private stable for many years after the retirement of George Lambton. Under the stewardship of Colledge Leader, Walter Earl and George Colling, the 'black, white cap' colours were rarely out of the frame for long. In 1963, the 18th Earl decided that Stanley House should become a public stable and a lease was granted to the extremely able and progressive figure of Bernard Van Cutsem, who trained for Lord Derby in addition to the impressive coterie of owners he had built up during his time at Graham Place. A successful decade later, Van Cutsem died and the property was sold to the young trainer, Gavin Pritchard-Gordon.

British racing's prodigal son, John Gosden.
(photo, Tony Edenden)

Stanley House, however, is the kind of place that requires a major patron, and after a relatively brief interregnum, the yard has once again been thrust into the limelight, through its purchase by Sheikh Mohammed. The effect on the Stanley House yard has been dramatic. It is rare, if not unique, in the hidebound, recession-hit milieu of British racing, to find a historic training establishment (stable really seems an inadequate description in this context) where the glories of the past are not only matched but surpassed by the present. If the Maktoum family were to leave no other trace to mark their time in British racing, the restoration and development of Stanley House Stables would stand as a fitting monument to their enthusiasm for the turf.

The man fortunate enough to have been chosen by Sheikh Mohammed to inherit the mantle of George Lambton, is John Gosden. As the son of Towser Gosden - by common consent, one of the shrewdest and most patient trainers in modern racing history - the younger Gosden can boast a significant racing pedigree, in addition to a fast-track early career that has long marked him out as a potential champion trainer. After working with no less a duo than Vincent O'Brien and Sir Noel Murless (in his last years at Warren Place), Gosden gained further experience on America's West Coast, where he rose to become one of America's leading trainers.

Although leaving a thriving business in the States was a wrench, the potential of a place like Stanley House in the hands of arguably the most important patron in world racing was limitless. Anyone who has visited the yard since its restoration and extension could not fail to be impressed by what has already been achieved. "Only someone like Sheikh Mohammed could have brought about the transformation of this place" according to Gosden. "Others might have been able to patch it up but a complete overhaul and extension on this scale would have been completely out of most people's reach". So extensive and ambitious were the Sheikh's plans for Stanley House that, for the first year of Gosden's tenure, the yard was "effectively a building site". The Sheikh and Gosden were both keen that the existing stable buildings be restored in every detail and that any new buildings should harmonize with the original.

Although Gosden is no slavish adherent of tradition for its own sake, he is a believer in the old yard's beauty and utility. "It is a beautiful facade and a very fine design. We've gone to great

The restored face of the main yard at Stanley House, a classic of Victorian stable design.

lengths to maintain its traditional appearance, keeping the black and white Lord Derby colours for the boxes and designing any new windows in the same style".

The boxes in the main yard are a traditional mixture of passage and outside boxes, the latter finding most favour with the trainer. "The passage boxes are very well built: very cool in summer and warm in winter and were built with high quality wood but horses are essentially gregarious, herd animals and seem to do better when they can see each other. They can develop a tendency to weave or box walk in isolation". The old yard is an atmospheric place redolent with the patina of age. Underneath the main archway is an evocative collection of horseshoes belonging to past winners, each surrounding a description of the event and the sum of money won. Tiny Hyperion, the Derby winner of 1933, is represented by a characteristically diminutive shoe, barely big enough to accommodate the relevant information.

Fit for a Sheikh's horses: the interior of one of the yard's airy barns.

From the working museum of the main yard's archway, it is possible to look out beyond the 'back 20', a subsidiary range of boxes contemporary with the main yard, to the extraordinary new complex of buildings built by Sheikh Mohammed. This consists of a series of three cathedral-like, L-shaped barns, beautifully light and airy thanks to glazed ridges, and a superbly constructed wooden covered ride, complete with lungeing rings. The buildings are practical, working structures, but because of the thoughtfulness of their design, their scale and the quality of the materials used, they have a grandeur that is quite in-keeping with the Stanley House tradition, a fact that pleases the trainer.

"They had to harmonize with the original buildings; we didn't want a concrete jungle out there. Sheikh Mohammed was particularly keen that the covered ride should not just look like a tin shed". The barns, too, are very far removed from the off-the-shelf American model and were designed by Gosden specifically with the English climate in mind. "U.S barns face outwards, whereas ours face in for obvious reasons, but there is plenty of natural light and they are very well ventilated, with plenty of fresh air circulating".

Gosden is keen on as natural environment as possible for the training and development of the horses in his care. "This is where the Europeans excel. Training in Britain and France is far more natural than in America. The training grounds are far more conducive to the development of a young horse. Nothing like the American system, where 2000 horses have to be exercised on the same dirt track between 5.30 and 9.30". This apart, Gosden believes that the British have a lot to learn from their transatlantic counterparts. "The Americans' attention to soundness is in a different league to ours, so that for an older horse that has come through its development problems, it would be hard to justify staying over here, as they have an excellent race programme for older horses and can keep them sound longer".

A small section of Stanley House's extensive horseshoe museum.

Like his father before him, John Gosden is unusually punctilious about every little detail concerning the well-being and development of his horses. "My father's influence would be in terms of attitude. He took infinite pains with a horse and was extraordinarily patient and caring. If they were pulling out and a black cloud appeared, they'd all be scurried back in again and he would stand at the window and wait until he thought that it had cleared".

"In those days you could afford to wait with a horse until it had reached its best at three or four. My father and George Todd would lay out a horse for a year. Leaving aside the economics of doing nothing with a horse for a year, you couldn't get the cash on today. All the big bookmakers are interested in is servicing an endless fruit machine of mug punters in the betting shops."

What would Towser Gosden make of trainers today? "He wouldn't like it with the pressurized lifestyle. He'd be shocked at the way we all run around with mobile phones sticking out of our pockets but, however desirable it may have been, the old pace of life would be impossible today. The days of two lots and lads showing their two horses are over I'm afraid."

The more traditional accommodation in the yard is a mixture of outside and (above) passage boxes.

Towser Gosden's final advice to his son before his untimely death was "whatever you do, don't become a trainer". The wily old Master of Heath House, Lewes may very well have been persuaded to change his mind had he been able to see his son ensconced at a revitalised Stanley House.

PROPRIETOR:
Sheikh Mohammed

PAST TRAINERS:
Hon.George Lambton; Colledge Leader; Frank Butters; Walter Earl; George Colling; Bernard Van Cutsem; Gavin Pritchard-Gordon

NOTABLE HORSES:
Keystone II; Canyon; Fair Isle; Hyperion; Tideway; Watling Street; Herringbone; Garden Path; Sun Stream; Alycidon; Swallow Tail; Park Top; Karabas; Sharpen Up; High Top; Mashaalah

OWNERS:
Sheikh Mohammed; Hamdan Al-Maktoum; Sheikh Ahmed Al-Maktoum; Sheikh Ahmed Bin Saeed Al-Maktoum; Lord Derby; Lord Hartington; Cheveley Park Stud; R. Sangster; Lord White of Hull; George Strawbridge; M.L. Oberstein; Robert Clay; Mrs M.M.C. Clark; Mrs Roger Waters; Mike Rutherford; Landon Knight; R.K. Eamer; W.S. Farish III; Saeed Manana; Mrs Sonia Rogers; Mrs Elizabeth Moran; Thomas.P. Tatham; Mrs Shirley.H. Taylor; David Thompson.

Brecongill, near Middleham.

Miss Sally Hall

There can be few yards in the north of England as steeped in racing history as Brecongill, latterly the home, stud and racing stable of that redoubtable northern horsewoman, Sally Hall. The present house and yard at Brecongill were built, on the site of a much earlier house, in the early part of the nineteenth century by one of the characters of the northern turf of that period, John Mangle, universally known as 'Crying Jackie' because of his inability to take defeat equably. The Leyburn-born Mangle had been a very successful jockey, winning the St.Leger in three consecutive years in the late eighteenth century, and then married the daughter of the Ashgill trainer, John Hoyle, from whom he inherited the yard. His string soon grew too big for Ashgill, so he decided to develop the neighbouring property, Brecongill, then a farm. Sadly, Mangle never saw his project come to fruition, as he was struck down by blindness in middle age and was forced to give up training.

The yard first achieved racing fame in the period 1830-49, when it became the stable of Thomas Dawson, the first of that great Scottish racing clan to venture south. He began training at Brecongill in 1830 at the age of 21 and despite his youth was mature enough to develop his own innovatory ideas. He disliked the then almost universal practice of sweating horses (ie: covering them in heavy rugs and hoods for exercise in order to sweat off excess flesh) and did away with the practice altogether. Much to the consternation of other local trainers who had laughed at the young man's presumption, Dawson achieved considerable success with his newfangled training methods, sending out the winners of the Oaks and the St Leger in 1842.

Sally Hall at the gates of Brecongill with Nicky Connorton and Silverlocks.

Later in the century, Brecongill became the home and later the training establishment of that legendary cock of the north, John Osborne, universally acknowledged as the best northern jockey of his century. The 'Middleham number' of the *Racing Illustrated* magazine in 1895 records that "nowhere can horses receive more careful attention than at Brecongill". By all accounts, Osborne was a scrupulously honest and charitable man, who never pushed his horses for short term gain, a tradition that has persisted down the years. A contemporary photograph shows a happy family group arranged casually in front of the ivy-clad house, the stone-walled stabling flanking the house on both sides. (Curiously, Brecongill would occupy an important place in any female history of the turf, even without Sally Hall. Ellen Chaloner, John Osborne's daughter, who was born at Brecongill, became the first woman permitted to hold a training licencse).

Brecongill, unchanged since the days of John Osborne.

The house has barely changed in the hundred years since. The ivy has, thankfully, been removed, to reveal the old house's attractive coursed rubble stonework, but otherwise, the layout is almost exactly the same. There is something of the time capsule about Brecongill, which lies in a secluded and sheltered hollow between the Low and High Moors in the parish of Coverham, well away from the bustle of Leyburn and Middleham. Although the surrounding hills shroud the house from the outside world, it is not really isolated at all but part of the tiny cluster of training establishments, comprising Tupgill, Ashgill and Spigot Lodge as well as Brecongill.

The most recent chapter in Brecongill's long history concerns the Hall family who, like so many in nothern racing, have been involved with horses, in various ways, for generations. Before they established themselves in racing circles, the Hall family name was well known throughout Yorkshire for the breeding of hackneys. Before the war, 'Charlie' W.A. Hall, Sally's uncle, turned his attention to the breeding and then the training of National Hunt horses, establishing quite a reputation at his farm at Towton, just outside Tadcaster. Among many good horses that he trained was Doorknocker, the winner of the 1956 Champion Hurdle. Sally's father, Tom, joined him in partnership at Towton, building up his own retinue of smart flat race horses.

Sally Hall grew up at Towton - "I was steeped in jumping and point-to-pointing" - and remembers fondly her Uncle Charlie's "patient training methods". Eventually, Sally's father, Tom Hall, that "unaffected, blunt Yorkshire farmer sportsman", as he was described in a contemporary newspaper article, decided to step out on his own.

After the war, Tom Hall was persuaded to buy Brecongill by his friend Matt Peacock, the famous Middleham trainer. The house had been requisitioned by the Army during the war and had briefly been the home of Noel Murless before he left to set up at Hambleton (Julie Cecil

Sally leads the string onto the Low Moor through the morning mist.

was born at Brecongill). Sally Hall remembers that "It had no electricity and the high ceilinged rooms were dark and heated by little Calor Gas stoves".

Tragically, Sally Hall's father, Tom, died soon after taking over at Brecongill and was succeeded by her other uncle, Sam, whose name was to become indivisibly associated with the yard over the next twenty years. As soon as she was old enough to leave school, Sally, who, by her own admission, had been a headstrong filly in her youth, running away from boarding school on more than one occasion so that she could be with her beloved horses, joined her Uncle Sam as assistant trainer. She had been making headlines in the racing press since the tender age of 12, when the horse she rode out for her uncle in her school holidays, the mercurial one-eyed miler Good Taste, only seemed to perform at his best when the trainer's niece was around.

At his peak, Sam Hall had 50-60 horses at Brecongill. Despite considerable success with two year olds, his niece believes he should be remembered for his patience: "he would always give a horse time to mature, which I hope is a characteristic I've inherited, and once he'd got the hang of them, they'd run well until they were ten".

Victorian 'Cock o' the North', John Osborne, Master of Brecongill.

A good case in point was Morecambe, a top-heavy gelding who never ran at two, but then set a record for the amount of money earned by a gelding, winning the Ebor, the Cesarewitch, the Timeform Gold Trophy and numerous other handicaps in a memorable career. Since Sam Hall's retirement, Sally has remained true to the traditional Hall virtues of patience and perseverance and been rewarded by a number of good and consistent performers, the most notable of which has been the appropriately named Hallgate.

Bought for a syndicate organised by the Doncaster bookie, Michael Geraghty, for 11,000 guineas, Sally describes him wryly as "the type bought to be a sharp little two year old to whip round Catterick". "He was a very correct horse but he was only small - about 14.2 - and he was not a good mover and used to slop along". Despite being beaten on his first three outings as a two year old, his trainer never lost faith, a trust that was repaid admirably when the brave little bay went on to become one of the top sprinters of his generation, and certainly the most popular.

Parts of the yard date from the seventeenth century.

Sally Hall's present string, like most of those situated away from the town, tend to use the High rather than the Low Moor for their exercise, a fifteen minute walk from the yard. For the horses based in Middleham itself, the walk to the High Moor is something of a trek but one regularly undertaken by some of the town-based trainers, notably Mark Johnston.

It is well worth the walk; the High Moor must be the most scenic and atmospheric setting in Britain for an exercise gallop. A mile and a half gallop around a rocky escarpment covered with weatherbeaten trees, bordered by dry stone walls, and punctuated by historic remnants like the old rubbing houses (in the nineteenth century, horses were galloped in heavy clothing in order to make them sweat, were rubbed down and then bled in the belief that the loss of weight through sweating and the thinning of the blood helped to achieve fitness). It feels like a racecourse transferred to the top of a mountain, a fact exploited by Chris Thornton's Shotgun, fourth in Shergar's Derby and Middleham's most recent Derby hopeful, who prepared for the Epsom race by working the 'wrong way round' the High Moor.

"Waiting for the good one to come along", as Sally Hall describes the trainer's lot, can be a positive pleasure in surroundings like these. Looking at Brecongill's paddocks, replete with familiar mares and those as yet unrealised bags of potential called foals, it would be hard to imagine a more idyllic lifestyle for a lover of horses.

NOTABLE HORSES:
Our Nell; Blue Bonnet; Good Taste; Morecambe;
Burns Trinity; King's Lane;
Fine Sun; Cool Decision; Silver Haze; Hallgate.

PAST TRAINERS:
John Mangle; Thomas Dawson; John Osborne; Fred Osborne;
Tom Hall; Sam Hall

OWNERS:
Lord Matthews; Hon.I.V. Matthews; R. Ogden; Mrs Joan Hodgson;
Miss Betty Duxbury; Mrs.T. Hall; J. Hanson; C. Platts;
G.W. Westgarth; W.G. Barker;
George Ward

KINGWOOD HOUSE, LAMBOURN.

MAJOR W.R.HERN C.V.O

COMMUTERS JOURNEYING ALONG the M4 between Swindon and Newbury can just catch a tantalising glimpse of what looks, to all intents and purposes, like a racecourse snaking its way across the Lambourn Downs. They are in fact gallops, 'Hamdan's gallops' as they are knowingly referred to by the locals in "the valley of the racehorse', where everyone seems to know at least something about racing.

It is here, in a yard adjacent to the famous old Derby gallops on Farncombe Down, that one of the most influential men in British racing, Sheikh Hamdan Al Maktoum, has installed the trainer of Nashwan and Dayjur, Major W.R.Hern, lately the tenant of the Queen's racing stables at West Ilsley.

Missing nothing, The Major scrutinizes the morning's work.

The Major is far too fly to be drawn into invidious comparisons between his brand new high-tec training establishment and the scene of his past triumphs. "This is newer" he says, with a gleam in his eye "and, anyway, comparisons are odious". In some ways, Major Hern's regime at Kingswood House is a continuation rather than a new beginning. Most of the staff have relocated the few miles across the Downs and some have even retained the tenancy of council houses in West Ilsley.

The atmosphere, too, of the new yard bears the imprint of Major Hern's personality. Although the Major plays down his role in the design and layout of the new yard, a number of his ideas have been incorporated. As might be expected of a military man, the yard is exceptionally well ordered and tightly disciplined. Security is a particular concern of the Major's. Just as at West Ilsley, a security guard is posted at the entrance to the yard overnight to discourage would-be nobblers, and photographs are banned in "sensitive areas". Ironically, one of the few proven cases of horse-doping in recent years was visited on one of Major Hern's horses, Bravefoot, at Doncaster, an incident that has redoubled the trainer's vigilance.

The facilities at Kingwood House, as one might expect of such a patron, are impressive. The old yard on the site, which was formerly occupied by Captain Mark Smyly, has been completely demolished and rebuilt to the Sheikh's specifications, with two symmetrical thirty box yards flanking a central collecting yard, complete with traditional clock tower. Everything exudes the slightly unreal newness of an estate of starter homes.

Although it is brand new, Kingwood House bears all the traditional hallmarks of a racing yard.

The traditional appearance of the buildings, however, belies the sophistication of the operation, which incorporates such sophisticated luxuries as a solarium; electronic treadmill and walk-through weighing room (for the horses) in addition to an immaculate covered ride; spacious lungeing ring; a permanent workshop and an on-site smithy. Even the feed room, where the all important oats are cleaned and crushed, has something of Cape Canaveral about it, with huge, chrome hoppers and dust extractors towering above the feed man, who is permanently employed to keep the tried and tested recipe of the horses' diet correct right down to the last oat.

Six furlongs straight across the downs.

At the time of writing, after eighteen months in situ at the new yard, Major Hern admits to "only just getting used to" his new surroundings, which, along with the state of the art facilities, also include the use of the nearby Farncombe Down gallops, which were acquired separately at the same time as the purchase of Kingwood House. The scope of these magnificent downland gallops, where Felstead and Windsor Lad, the Derby winning horses of 1928 and '34, were trained (by Ossie Bell and Marcus Marsh respectively) has propelled Kingwood House into the premier league of training establishments.

Trotting home.

"They've taken a bit of getting used to because you have to go through all the seasons of the year before you can really say that you've got the hang of them but I've a lad, Brian Procter, who has ridden work on them for years and knows them very well, so we weren't completely in the dark".

In character, the gallops appear very different from those at West Ilsley, with less inclines but Major Hern disagrees "If anything, they're a bit stiffer and there is a beautiful cover of grass". In addition to a round gallop of a mile and a quarter, there is a valley gallop of a mile and a spectacular all weather gallop, which stretches picturesquely along the crest of a hill for six straight furlongs.

Closer to home, on a large field adjacent to the yard is another seven furlong all weather gallop built, to the Major's specifications, on the round with a furlong pull-up. "It's at least fourteen feet across so that three horses can work upsides comfortably and even four at a push". Despite being wheelchair-bound since his hunting accident, the Major is never more at home than when supervising work on the gallops, scrutinising everything with customary intensity from the passenger seat of his four wheel drive jeep.

As we watch successive groups of younger horses cantering and trotting around the all weather during third lot, the Major points out a half sister to Nashwan in one group (then unraced but subsequently installed as a leading fancy for the Oaks after winning her maiden at Newmarket) and a half sister to Dayjur in another. Soon, Nashwan and Dayjur's own progeny will begin to appear.

Despite the change of scenery, it is inevitable that in a yard superintended by a living legend, the events of today are enshrined by memories of the past and of a proud history of achievement, but with the bloodlines at the Sheikh's disposal, the past virtually guarantees a continuity of success.

PROPRIETOR:
Shadwell Estate

PAST TRAINERS:
Yard (Capt. R.M. Smyly);
Gallops (Capt. O.M. Bell; Marcus Marsh)

OWNERS:
Sheikh Hamdan Al Maktoum;
Sheikh Ahmed Al Maktoum;
Sheikh Mohammed; Lord Rotherwick; Lord Weinstock;
Sir John Astor; Lord Chelsea;
Mrs Hugh Dalgety; Mr R.D. Hollingsworth; Vijay Mallya;
Mrs M. Wettermark; R.J. McReery;
Mrs Roger Waters;
Dr.G. Rausing & Dr.B. Rausing

Hodcott House, West Ilsley.

Lord Huntingdon

NEVITABLY, MEMORIES OF Major Hern and a whole host of equine personalities loom large over the Queen's racing stables at Hodcott House, West Ilsley. They must be a hard act to follow. For the last quarter of a century, the racing appendage to this otherwise sleepy Berkshire village has been indivisibly associated with turf success.

The yard itself at Hodcott House comes as something of a surprise to the uninitiated. It is clearly not a purpose-built racing stable at all but a small, unassuming farm that has evolved and mutated into the impressive training complex that it now is, over a number of years. In the last century, racing was combined with the principal business of farming. It was not until the end of the First World War that the sole business of the estate came to be the training of racehorses, under the direction of that famous trainer of stayers, Captain Gooch, who, like Major Hern half a century later, was seriously injured in a hunting accident. (Marcus Marsh, the trainer of Palestine and Tulyar, was the Captain's first assistant after his accident).

Only a small section of the present day yard dates from prior to that period: a rather gloomy bachelors' quarters known as 'The Seven' where the occasionally temperamental older colts are presently housed in a corner of the main yard. The worn sloping brick of the floor and the patina of the old boxes, stained and restained year after year, testify to its age as can Major Hern, who remembers former trainer Geoffrey Barling (who was born at Hodcott House in 1902, and whose father, Frank, trained there at the turn of the century) telling him that Hornet's Beauty - winner of all fifteen of his races in 1911 - once stood in the Sevens. The rest of the boxes in the yard are either conversions of existing farm buildings or are much later additions.

Lord Huntingdon and Bellinger on Winterdown.

Most of the later building work, including the lads' hostel and bungalows, dates from 1962, when the yard was purchased by the notable racehorse owner and society figure, the Hon. J.J. (Jakie) Astor, who installed Major Hern as trainer in succession to Jack Colling, who ended a long association with the Astor family, when he retired from training in the same year.

Just as the yard grew in stages, so did the trainer's house, which is separated from the yard itself by a pretty, tree-fringed pond and garden. The odd panel of timber framing reveals Hodcott House's origins as a modest farmhouse, but in the last one hundred and fifty years it has been periodically extended until now it is something like three times its original size. Unlike Lord

The trainer's home, Hodcott House, is sixteenth century in origin and has been extended gradually over the years.

Huntingdon, who lives at Hodcott House, Major Hern never lived in the main house. It was occupied at the time of his arrival at West Ilsley by his predecessor, Jack Colling, and once the opportunity arose to move in, the Major preferred to remain in The Old Rectory in the village, which he had converted to the newly changed circumstances of his life after the hunting accident, which left him wheelchair-bound.

Hodcott House, West Ilsley has changed patrons twice since Jakie Astor took the yard effectively beyond the means of most trainers seeking to own their own training establishment. In Brigadier Gerard's annus mirabilis, 1971, the estate was sold to Lady Anne Sobell, in whose family it remained until the multi-million pound sale of the Queen's brilliant filly, Height of Fashion, financed Her Majesty's purchase of the yard from which she had enjoyed such success.

The inner sanctum at Hodcott House is the 'Security Yard', so called because a guard has traditionally been positioned, in a military-style sentry box, at its entrance overnight in the build up to big races. All the classic-entered horses at West Ilsley have been stationed there in those nervous preparatory weeks. Over the years, stable lads have etched the names of their famous charges into the brickwork around the boxes. So many famous names in fact that barely a brick remains untouched around some. Major Hern's successor at West Ilsley, Lord Huntingdon (formerly Willie Hastings Bass) has erected more permanent memorials in the shape of brass plaques bearing their names. Far from being intimidated by such graphic reminders of an illustrious past, the new incumbent at West Ilsley thinks it will serve as encouragement. "It's rather nice to have a continuous reminder of decent horses".

While manifestly respectful of the yard's history, Lord Huntingdon is by no means superstitious, laughing off any suggestion that the horses positioned in these boxes are put there for any equine fairy dust from the past that might rain down on them. "I'm afraid it's not quite as easy as that".

After just two seasons at West Ilsley, there are signs that the ghosts of the past are already being laid. The West Ilsley roll of honour was extended in Lord Huntingdon's opening season at the yard by that gallant stayer Indian Queen, who became the first mare since Gladness in 1958 to win the Ascot Gold Cup, an achievement made all the remarkable because she was in foal (to Night Jar) at the time. With around eighty horses in the yard at present, twenty five of which are owned by the Queen, West Ilsley looks set to resume its position high in the league table of success. Already, in combination with the Queen's other trainer, Ian Balding, Lord Huntingdon has enabled Her Majesty to beat her previous best total of winners in a season.

As so often in racing, that elusive and precious quantity, 'success', has its roots firmly grounded in practicality. Major Hern's phenomenal record is doubtless due in no small part to his universally acknowledged skills as a trainer, but the facilities he had at West Ilsley certainly were no hindrance. The move to Hodcott House, West Ilsley has manifestly improved Lord Huntingdon's 'luck'. In the year before the move, his team managed 16 winners, earning just over £100,000 in prize money. In the season following the move, the number of winners had increased to 31 and the prize money to over £400,000.

If anything can be said to be the key to the success of West Ilsley, it must be the range and quality of the well-established gallops. In character they are similar to the principal gallops at nearby Lambourn, springy downland grass and lots of stamina building climbs on the slopes of the Ridgeway. Unsurprisingly, the surrounding land is dominated by jumping yards. Next door at East Ilsley is Simon Sherwood's Summerdown yard and in the other direction, at East Hendred, Andy Turnell's gallops can be found. In addition to the grass gallops, there is a woodchip gallop and an equitrack, which means, in theory at least, that even on the most frostbound mornings of winter, with the judicious use of a power harrow, work can still proceed. In recent years, with the advent of all weather racing, this has proved invaluable, leading to the slightly incongruous sight of the Queen's colours being carried to victory in maiden races at Southwell.

The royal colours are prepared for an outing.

For Lord Huntingdon, positioned halfway up Winterdown on his champion show cob, Bellinger, watching third lot cantering up

Epicentre of the action at Hodcott House: the security yard.

the woodchip gallop, West Ilsley seems a long way from Newmarket. "Of course at Newmarket, there was the watered gallop and some would say being at headquarters is useful from the point of view of work riders, but it's wonderful here. On a nice summer's morning there's just you, the larks and the horses in all this unspoilt countryside".

PAST TRAINERS:
Frank Barling; Captain Gooch; Eric Stedall;
R.J. Colling; Major W.R. Hern.

PAST ASSISTANTS:
Marcus Marsh; David Murray-Smith; Ian Cocks; Alex Scott

NOTABLE HORSES:
Hornet's Beauty; Ambiguity; Provoke; Brigadier Gerard; Highclere; Bustino;
Dunfermline; Troy; Henbit; Bireme; Sun Princess; Cut Above; Ela Mana Mou;
Petoski; Nashwan; Dayjur Drum Taps.

OWNERS:
Her Majesty The Queen; Lord Carnarvon; Lord Weinstock; Lord Derby;
Lord Halifax; Sultan Mohammed; Henryk de Kwiatkowski; Sir Gordon Brunton;
M.L. Oberstein; Lady Newman; Mrs Ian Pilkington;
George Mooratoff; Lord Weinstock;
Hon.S. Weinstock; K.H. Fischer; Stanley J. Sharp; Mrs M. Coker;
J. Rose; James Wigan; Lewis M. Schott; Sir Michael Sandberg;
Mrs Evan Williams; Yoshio Asakawa; J.T. Thomas; E.J. Loder;
Maverick Productions Ltd

Thirty Acre Barn, Epsom.

Geoff Lewis

The racecourse and training grounds on the Downs at Epsom are an oasis in an otherwise featureless suburban sprawl that has engulfed most of the small villages that once punctuated the unspoilt countryside. One of the few pockets of old Surrey that remains is a patch of rural land that has resisted development, at Headley, half a mile from the Derby start, across a small valley.

Its survival is largely due to the presence of a number of racing stables, whose paddocks and private training grounds have prevented the encroachment of yet more housing. At the end of a long lane in Headley is one of Epsom's most famous training establishments, Thirty Acre Barn, a secluded spot, which first came to the notice of the racing public in the early 1950s, when it became the home of one of Epsom's favourite sons, Staff Ingham.

Ingham was born and bred in South London and served his apprenticeship with Stanley Wootton at Treadwell House in Epsom in the 1920s. Wootton is rightly remembered as the man who ensured the future of Epsom as a training centre by assigning the Walton Downs work grounds he had bought for £35,000 in 1924, to the Levy Board. Wootton's stable was a well known source of top jockeys and his one time apprentice Ingham confirmed that reputation by becoming one of the top jump jockeys of his generation. Unlike many of his weighing room colleagues, Ingham was sufficiently shrewd to get out before he was stretchered out and took up training while still a relatively young man in the late 1930s.

The Second World War interrupted Ingham's new career but saw him rise to the rank of Wing Commander in the RAF. When hostilities ceased, Ingham looked around for a place to train and decided upon Thirty Acre Barn, which he bought for the princely sum of £15,000. Within a very few years, Ingham had established a considerable reputation under both codes and controlled one of the largest and most successful strings in Epsom.

Staff Ingham's son Tony, who briefly succeeded him at Thirty Acre Barn, remembers his father from a professional perspective as "a man with a very good eye for a horse, regardless of pedigree. He bought Chantry for 35 guineas and the horse went on to win the Cesarewitch. Persian Bold was bought for under £20,000 and I sold him for half a million". Although he is reluctant to make any specific comparisons with any of today's trainers, Tony Ingham believes that his father has no current rival, when it comes to the preparation of two year olds. "None of the two year old trainers today could hold a candle to him".

Epsom's favourite adopted son, Geoff Lewis.

Silver Wisp at home.

Staff Ingham was equally shrewd in his dealings with the bookmakers, a talent inherited by his son, who remembers some of the coups with awed respect: "He won fantastic amounts in his time, most of it when I was still at school. One of his greatest coups was with his own horse Chantry in the 1953 Cesarewitch. It was backed from 66-1 ante post to 4-1 favourite on the day". Although he has now given up training, Tony has by no means severed his connections with racing. He is now a professional gambler and runs a private tipping service, which is advertised in the national sporting press. Waging war against the old enemy, according to Ingham, is considerably more difficult today than in the days of Chantry: "It was easier to get money on then. Bookmakers were bookmakers, not accountants like they are today".

Tony Ingham gave up training after a year and a half in his father's old yard, selling it to a man who has become almost synonymous with training in Epsom, Geoff Lewis. The pugnacious, silver-haired Welshman began his long and distinguished riding career barely a mile from Thirty Acre Barn, at the Epsom stables of Ron Smyth, riding his first winner at the local spring meeting in 1953 at the age of eighteen. Throughout his riding career, he maintained his connections with the area and was a frequent visitor to Thirty Acre Barn.

"Staff was the best trainer of two year olds I've ever come across and a great trainer of any other horse come to that. In many ways he was unlucky: he should have won the St Leger with Just Great, but the horse whipped round at the start". "In many ways, Staff was the ideal person to follow on from here. It's no good modelling yourself on Noel Murless, when you're working with moderate tackle. I learnt a lot from him - litle things like not to worry about a horse sweating up. I remember him saying 'they're entitled to sweat - it shows they're taking an interest'."

Lewis has become something of an unpaid public relations consultant for Epsom, extolling its virtues at every opportunity: "It's just fashion that says Newmarket is the place to send a classic horse. If you take away the private gallops at Manton, Kingsclere, Whitsbury and Beckhampton, the Epsom work grounds are the best in the country. It's not overworked like Newmarket. Ask any work rider and he'll tell you, it compares with anything Newmarket or Lambourn can offer. I don't go out of here in the winter".

Lewis himself, of course, is the best advertisement for the virtues of training at Epsom. With fearsome levels of hard work and exacting standards for his staff - a notice on the tack room wall declares that anyone found guilty of incompetence will be given a week's notice - Lewis' training career has always maintained an upwards curve. The Lewis string are always the first on the Downs in the morning, rising before the dawn to get the best ground.

Horses trained at Epsom quickly get used to coping with traffic.

In recent seasons, Lewis has consistently confounded those who doubted Epsom's ability to compete. He has put his money where his mouth is, too, backing himself succesfully, at long odds, to reach seemingly impossible targets of winners. In recent years, he has more than doubled the number of winners produced by the yard, from 25 to 50 plus.

The rise in the quantity of winners emanating from the Lewis camp has been more than matched by an increase in quality, giving the lie to the idea that top horses can only be trained in Newmarket or Berkshire. As so often in racing, this has not happened by accident. Lewis has made a deliberate policy of buying a better class of horse at the sales, paying a bit more than in previous years on behalf of owners prepared to invest for Group race and classic success. A few seasons ago this may have seemed nothing more than a pipedream, but the performances of the Robins' Silver Wisp and Silver Wizard have made quite a few people eat their words. What price a Group One winner from the yard in? Ladbrokes are unlikely to offer 50-1 about that.

PAST TRAINERS:
Staff Ingham; Tony Ingham

NOTABLE HORSES:
Just Great; Chantry; Philoctotes; Porto Bello;
Persian Bold; Perion;
Point of Light; Silver Wisp; Silver Wizard

OWNERS:
Ken Higson; Shirley Robins; Wing Commander Hugh Tudor;
A.J. Richards; Lady McIndoe; Victor Chandler; P.D. Savill;
A. Midani; P.R. Pritchard; Vic Fatah; Nigel Morris;
Mrs David Barker; T.K.Laidlaw; Ronnie Corbett; Mrs. D. Hayes;
N. Topche; J. Ward Hill; H. Kaya; Roy Bays;
M.J.E. Thornhill; R.V. Wright;
N. Bedack; Jackie Ward Ramos

The Durdans, Epsom.

Joe Naughton

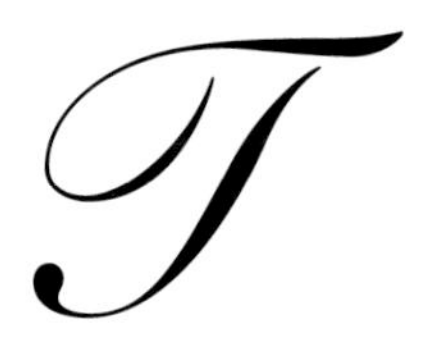

HERE ARE RACEHORSES once again at The Durdans, Epsom. After years of dereliction and decay, during which time the future of the historic stable buildings was in some doubt, a young trainer, Joe Naughton, has effected a transformation that will please anyone with even a passing interest in turf history.

It was more than a century ago that Archibald Philip Primrose, Fifth Earl of Rosebery, reluctant Liberal Prime Minister 1894-5 and enthusiastic owner/breeder of three Derby winners, made 'The Durdans' one of the landmarks of the English Turf. Racing history on the estate goes back even further, to Amato, the Derby winner of 1838, trained on the Downs by Ralph Sherwood for Sir Gilbert Heathcote, but it is the association with the Rosebery dynasty that ensured its lasting fame.

Despite the seriousness of his interest in politics, the Turf was always Lord Rosebery's consuming passion, his 'other life'. When threatened by the University authorities at Oxford with expulsion on the grounds that ownership of a racehorse was not consistent with the life of an undergraduate, the young Archibald (who had then yet to succeed to his title) wrote to his mother: 'Dear Mother, I have left Oxford. I have secured a house in Berkeley Square; and I have bought a horse to win the Derby. Your affectionate Archie'.

The old yard at the Durdans. (Racing Illustrated)

The horse, Ladas, went on to finish last in the Derby of 1869 (after being backed heavily at odds of 66-1). Twenty five years later, in the year of his brief premiership, Lord Rosebery won his first Derby with a horse nostalgically named Ladas II in memory of that first disastrous attempt. Delight at the PM's victory was not universal; there were mutterings in nonconformist sections of the Liberal party that owning racehorses was a sign of flippancy and lack of seriousness. Lord Rosebery retorted that he had owned unsuccessful racehorses for years without incurring any complaint.

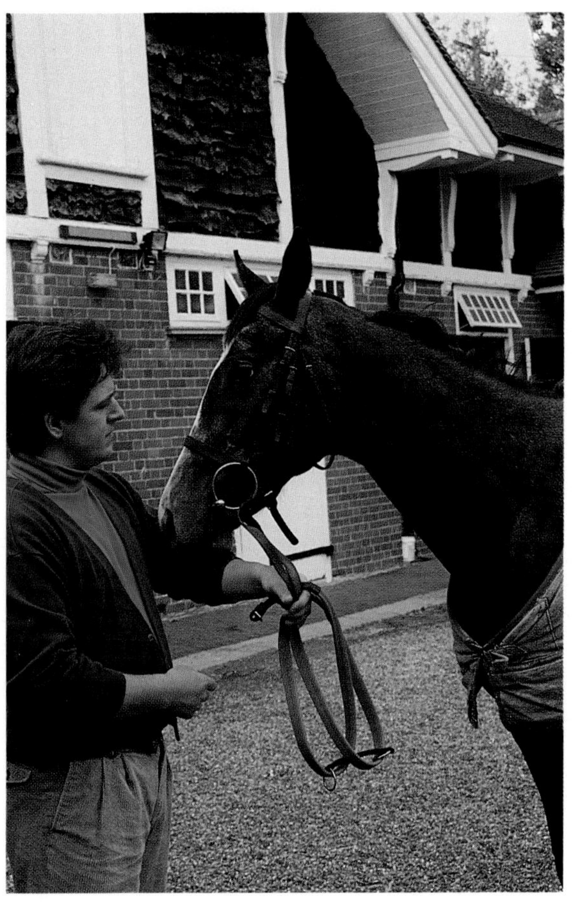

Joe Naughton and Call Me Blue.

Now that success on the racecourse had finally arrived, it came in spades. The next year, Lord Rosebery won the Derby again with the much less keenly fancied Sir Visto. But cruelly, equine success accompanied political failure: in the same year, the Liberal party suffered the worst electoral defeat in its history.

Although he had left the centre stage of politics, Rosebery remained an influential and popular figure, not least because of his enthusiastic patronage of the Turf.

After Rosebery's third Derby triumph with Cicero in 1905, a huge party was thrown at The Durdans, to which a considerable proportion of the local population were invited, entertained by three different bands playing in the grounds. In those days, the paddock and the parade ring at Epsom formed part of the Durdans estate and, on racedays, the earl would progress in his coach and four through the magnificent wrought iron gates of the house, along a broad tree-lined route to the course, watch the race and return, without ever leaving his own property. In later life, Rosebery became something of a recluse and eccentric, venturing out at night to sit in his carriage to listen to the nightingales in the woods by the elaborate graves of his beloved Derby winners.

Although most of Rosebery's horses were bred at 'Durdans' and 'came home' when not in training, they were sent away to be trained. Rosebery was a notoriously difficult and demanding owner who quickly became disenchanted with a losing trainer. This is clearly reflected in the number of trainers he employed during his years as an owner, involving most of the major names of the period, including William Walters; Percy Peck; Sam Darling; Walter Nightingall; Richard Dawson and Frank Hartigan.

Although he was captivated by the atmosphere and characters of the racecourse as a young man, often gambling huge sums of money (£1698 in one day at the Doncaster Leger meeting of 1867) Lord Rosebery's principal pleasure in racing was the enjoyment of his horses at home: "that most delightful furniture of any park or enclosure, the brood mare and the foal".

Named after Lord Rosebery's third Derby winner, Cicero Stables have been restored to their former glory.

This was reflected in the grand manner of their accommodation at The Durdans. From the rustic 'swiss cottage' boxes of the main yard, named Cicero Stables after Lord Rosebery's third Derby winner, to the grandeur of the indoor riding school and the picturesque paddocks, a horse at the Durdans was conspicuously well treated.

The present incumbent, Joe Naughton, for some years Barry Hills' assistant at the equally historic Manton, cannot believe his good fortune at having 'The Durdans' as his first address as a trainer in his own right. "As soon as I drove into the place, even though it was run-down, I fell in love with it. I'd been looking at yards in the Hamilton Road in Newmarket but as soon as I came here, I knew there was no comparison".

One of the most famous names in turf history.

Naughton has moved into the heart of the yard himself, converting part of the main stable block into a small cottage, appropriately called Cicero Cottage. The impressive high-ceilinged dining room was formerly a derelict feed room. It is very much a hands-on operation at The Durdans these days, with Joe's wife, Jo, doing the secretarial work as well as riding out and Joe Naughton combining the roles of trainer and head man, driving the horsebox and feeding every one of his small string of twenty seven horses himself, an aspect of the job he clearly enjoys.

More like a cathedral than a building for horses: the magnificent covered ride at The Durdans.

The contrast between the small scale of Naughton's training operation and the relative grandeur of the surroundings is not lost on the young trainer himself. The 50 acres of mature, tree-lined paddocks stretching from the gates of the main house to the racecourse and the spectacular indoor riding school (the only one in Epsom) must be the envy of most trainers in the country. The latter is the size of a small cathedral, with high ceilings and exposed beams to match. It contains an impressive balustraded viewing platform, where Lord Rosebery and guests could watch yearlings being broken.

Emulating the success of such a distinguished past will be immensely difficult; without a major patron and in a straitened economic climate, Joe Naughton has already achieved much in getting this far. One thing is for certain, there can be few more atmospheric and historic places in England to have a horse in training.

NOTABLE HORSES:
Amato; Ladas II;
Sir Visto; Cicero

PAST TRAINERS:
B. Whelan

OWNERS:
T.O'Flaherty; Mark Everett; John Redmond; Michael Everett;
G.Wiltshire; Jim Naughton; R.Popely; Derek Borrows;
Mrs Marilyn Lipman; Mrs.P.Payne; Mrs J.A.Prescott;
M.A.Edgington; Gerald Murray; B.Walker;
L.Mitten; A.Jessop; G.Anthony;
Drofmor Racing; Mrs S.Sheldon

Heath House, Newmarket.

Sir Mark Prescott

If you believed in reincarnation, Sir Mark Prescott could be Tregonwell Frampton, Queen Anne's 'Keeper of the Running Horses' and the first recorded trainer on the site of the present Heath House, reborn. A coursing, gamefowl-breeding sportsman of the old school, Sir Mark Prescott Bt, is something of a throwback in all but his training methods, which are set firmly in the twentieth century and which have earned him a reputation as "the professional's professional". A fellow trainer once said to me that he would "never claim one of Mark Prescott's because you'd have the devil of a job improving them".

Antiquarian of racing history that he is, the Tregonwell Frampton comparison is his own. "I suppose, from the print I've seen of him, with a dog at his feet and a bird on a table by his side that he might have approved of me" adding wryly, "but I'm not so sure about Mat Dawson. He'd have said what's he been doing with all these horses the last twenty three seasons and not one classic winner!"

The yard is topped off with a hare and hound weathercock.

It was the aforementioned Mat Dawson that established Heath House as one of the landmarks of the British turf. During his nineteen seasons at the yard, with the legendary Fred Archer as stable jockey for most of them, Dawson won an extraordinary eighteen classics, in addition to training perhaps the greatest horse Newmarket has ever seen (and certainly the greatest horse never to win a classic) in St Simon.

It would be no exaggeration to say that Dawson, a canny and independent-minded Scot, did more than any other single figure to establish what we understand today as the role of the professional public trainer. Although he had major patrons throughout the years of his greatest success, Lord Falmouth and the Duke of Portland most notable among them, he took the view, now widely accepted if not always practiced, that as a professional trainer, paid for his expertise, he should have the last word in the training of the horses.

Such was Dawson's success, that his authority was soon established, and the stable strength grew, from a limited number of horses stabled

A coursing, gamefowl-breeding sportsman of the old school: Sir Mark Prescott Bt.

in boxes behind the main house - an imposing Georgian dwelling, now demolished - to a huge string, stabled all over Newmarket in overspill yards and in a large new range, built in 1881, which now constitutes the main part of the modern Heath House set-up.

The present Heath House, which Sir Mark describes as "a hideous redbrick Victorian thing" was built in 1885 as the trainer's house for Mat Dawson's successor, his nephew, George Dawson. The stable patron at the time was the Duke of Portland, who used old Heath House as his Newmarket residence, the architectural shift reflecting the change in status of the Heath House trainer. For, unlike his uncle, George Dawson was very much a private trainer, employed by a syndicate of aristocratic owners, consisting of the Duke of Portland and the Lords Hastings, Crewe and Londonderry.

A host of colourful racing characters have occupied Heath House since the Dawson era ended in 1900 including the pugnacious American Jack Huggins, who trained Volodyovski, the Derby winner of 1901, and Jack Waugh, Sir Mark Prescott's immediate predecessor and former boss, who could claim a direct link to the glory days of the Victorian era through his uncle Dawson Waugh, whose godfather (hence the name) was none other than Mat Dawson.

Jack Waugh built up the stable strength from a relatively small twenty horses to about sixty on his retirement, uniting Heath House with the neighbouring yard of Osborne House (famous as the home of Ellen Chaloner, the first woman ever to be granted a training licence), so that when Sir Mark Prescott assumed control of the yard in 1970, he inherited a thriving concern. "In those days, most of the leading trainers had around 50-60 horses. Sam Armstrong, who had about 80, was thought to have far too many".

In 1970, Newmarket was very much in the hands of a rather elderly postwar generation of trainers: "I was the youngest by 19 years. I think Johnny Winter was the next youngest". Now,

Straight out onto the Heath with no roads to cross.

23 years on, Sir Mark Prescott has become one of the elder statesmen at Headquarters, and is the longest serving trainer in the town, bar Tom Jones. It is a longevity that Sir Mark Prescott puts down to retaining enthusiasm: "a lot of my colleagues lose interest in training the ordinary horse but I find the whole process of finding the right race for a horse that can only win off a mark of 55 endlessly fascinating".

There is nobody training in England at present that knows the racing calendar like Sir Mark Prescott, the man who pioneered the plundering of northern races, placing that tough two year old Spindrifter to win 13 races in a season around the northern gaff tracks and whose horses won seven of the first nine claimers to be run in Britain. Before the advent of claimers, amateur condition races, now a rarity, were what Sir Mark describes as his 'loophole'.

Shrewd placing might be one characteristic of the Prescott regime but another factor that helps to tip the scales back in the favour of this largely small-owner stable is the degree of care that the inmates receive. Sir Mark Prescott has developed the facilities at the modern Heath House to such an extent that it must be the best appointed fifty box yard in Newmarket, if not the country. In a relatively limited land area, typical of the more established town yards in Newmarket, Sir Mark has installed the kind of luxury trappings that one associates with much larger establishments: a specially commissioned swimming pool, complete with a sand pit and drying pens, a solarium and a quite magnificent covered ride that opens up directly onto the immediately adjacent Heath - "We are exactly equi-distant from the farthest gallop on racecourse side and Bury side, so you have access to just about every training surface imaginable" - at the pressing of a button.

Every last piece of construction and floor covering has been mulled over with the painstaking attention to detail that is typical of the man and his methods. This is no mere indulgence: the current Master of Heath House, like Mat Dawson before him, believes health and the prevention of accident and disease to be the key to contemporary racing success. Walking

The pool: a masterpiece of space management.

around evening stables at Heath House, it is strikingly apparent what a palpably healthy, well behaved and well groomed collection of animals the Prescott string is. It is no wonder that they perform so consistently and so well.

PAST TRAINERS:
Tregonwell Frampton; Mat Dawson; George Dawson; Jack Huggins; A.Ferguson; Gordon Sadler; Basil Jarvis; Fred Butters; Captain Tommy Hogg; Jack Waugh.

NOTABLE HORSES:
Kingcraft; Atlantic; Spinnaway; Silvio; Melton; St Simon; Ayrshire; Donovan; Mrs Butterwick; Volodyovski; Almiranta; Amerigo; Matador; Arabian Night; Spindrifter; Misty Halo; Case Law; Chicmond; Haarlow; Teeming Shore; Arpero.

OWNERS:
Lord Derby; Prince Fahd Salman; Lady Fairhaven; P.G.Goulandris; Mrs David Thompson; Maj.Gen Sir George Burns; Saeed Manana; W.E.Sturt; Capt.J.Macdonald-Buchanan; Pinnacle Racing Stable; G.E.Shouler; Graham Rock; Mrs R.A.Johnson; D.N.Hoult; Mrs L.Burnet; Neil Greig; Mrs F.R.Watts; Hesmonds Stud; Pin Oak Stable; G.Moore; A.R.C.Finn; L.A.Larratt; P.Mollins;Garth Insoll; Mrs C.R.Philipson; G.D.Waters; Miss Elizabeth Aldous; J.E. Fitzroy-Newdegate; C. Kaars-Sypesteyn; Cyril Humphris; P.J. McSwiney; Ivan Allen; A. Down; D. Ashforth; Richard Dedman; C. Jenkins; H. Moszkowicz; J. Rowles; A.E.T.Mines; Seikh Ahmed Bin Saeed Al Maktoum

Hurgill Lodge, Richmond.

Bill Watts

INETEENTH CENTURY RACEGOERS at Richmond in North Yorkshire would have travelled up the Hurgill Road past the spot where the gates of Hurgill Lodge now stand, on their way from the town's railway station to the remotely sited racecourse on the Low Moor.

Hurgill Lodge looks for all the world as though it dates from the era when Voltigeur won the only race of his two year old career at Richmond, his local track, but, in reality, the trainer's house and yard are a tasteful latterday pastiche, built in 1937 to the instructions of the 2nd Marquis of Zetland for his private trainer, Harry Peacock.

Richmond's racecourse, of course, has long gone, its distance from the town one of the contributory factors in its demise, but the tradition of racing in the area had persisted, even before Hurgill Lodge was constructed. The racecourse had continued in use, and is still used today, as gallops, by the town's small community of trainers, who worked their horses around the tight turns of the old track in sight of the ever more forlorn-looking remains of John Carr of York's fine old grandstand.

At the height of the summer, when the old racecourse ground begins to dry up, the horses traditionally adjourn to a stretch of ground on the High Moor, peaty moorland turf, where the

Bill Watts' pride and joy, Teleprompter, who, even at the age of twelve, still acts as a lead horse on the gallops.

Bill Watts watching his string at work with the decaying Richmond grandstand as a background.

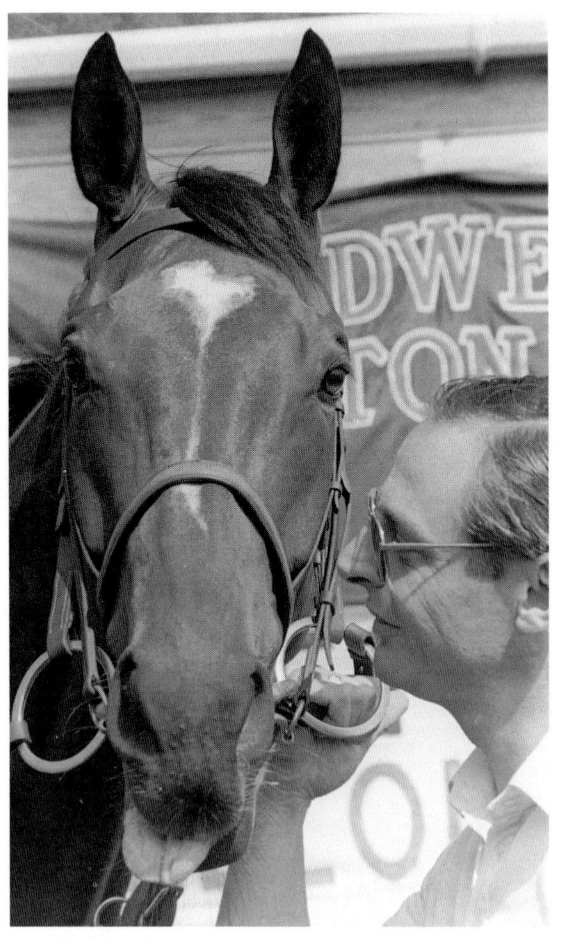

Teleprompter after winning the Arlington Million in 1985.

famous aristocratic matches of the eighteenth century took place, within sight of Aske Hall, seat of Hurgill Lodge's original patron, the Marquis of Zetland.

The present incumbent at Hurgill Lodge and only the fourth person ever to train there is Bill Watts, scion of the great Watts racing dynasty, who has now been living in his North Yorkshire second home for over twenty years. Hurgill Lodge is a fine place in which to live and train, modern enough to be spacious and convenient but attractively traditional in appearance and vernacular in character. The setting is airy and quiet with stunning views from the paddocks over Swaledale and the well-preserved old market town of Richmond. The peace of this delightful place is only disturbed whenever a Hurgill Lodge runner wins a race, a fact commemorated by a quick peal from a bell that hangs on the side of the main house.

Bill Watts trained in Newmarket for a time after leaving his father's employ, but has never regretted the move to Yorkshire. "I think I've proved that if you have the horses they can be trained as well up here as anywhere. I enjoy going racing but I'm a bit of a loner, I suppose and I do like to be able to come back here and be left alone". Success was quick in coming. Mrs Richard Stanley's brilliant filly, Waterloo, won the Queen Mary and the Cheveley Park in Bill Watts' first season at Hurgill Lodge, followed by the 1,000 Guineas in the second. Richmond was back on the map, and the racing press was full of the exploits of this latest member of the Watts dynasty bringing the glory days back to North Yorkshire.

Such reporting was typically premature. In attempting to maintain a high class string of horses in the unfashionable north, Bill Watts has been swimming against the tide for the last twenty years. Given such adverse circumstances, he has done remarkably well to continue to attract the support he does from distinguished owners such as Sheikh Mohammed and Robert Sangster. He has also continued to enjoy the patronage of Lord Derby, whose family have a connection with the Watts family dating back to 1955, when Bill's father became Lord Derby's private trainer.

It was this longstanding and fruitful association that produced perhaps the most popular horse seen at Richmond since Voltigeur, namely that durable gelding, Teleprompter. Unlike many of the best flat horses, whose brilliance is allowed to shine only for the very briefest of periods, Teleprompter seemed to be around for years, a picture of courage and determination and a walking advertisement for the virtues of Richmond as a place to keep horses healthy.

Even in his retirement, Teleprompter still comes back to the yard every year - "he still thinks he's in training" jokes Bill Watts - and in his twelfth year, looks in terrific shape, nearly pulling the arms off his lad on the gallops as he leads the string. His trainer has astonishing recall of the old horse's career, from Willie Carson's description of him as a 'big boat' on dismounting after his first outing at Doncaster to freeze frame accounts of his triumphs, great and small.

One ring for a winner.

Significantly, Bill Watts describes his principal feeling on Teleprompter achieving his famous victory in the Arlington Million as "relief". The daring nature of the venture, not to mention the expense and the fact that Bill Watts had stuck his neck out in suggesting the race in the first place meant that the stakes were high. Unlike the silver spoon brigade at Newmarket, there is no massive influx of choice yearlings at Hurgill Lodge to underwrite next year's classic entries.

Bill Watts has continued to walk the racing tightrope with panache ever since, always seeming to pull one out of the bag at the opportune moment. Colway Bold's triumph in the £140,000 Goffs Premier Challenge at the Curragh in 1991 with Lester Piggott on board was a timely one for the yard (the bell was rung with particular vehemence that night) and Satank's victory for Robert Sangster in the Windsor Castle at Royal Ascot justified the Master of Manton's continued (albeit small-scale) patronage of the north.

Who knows, with ten Sangster horses in the yard rather than one, Bill Watts might have to employ a permanent bell-ringer at Hurgill Lodge.

PAST TRAINERS:
H.D Peacock; G.O.Fenningworth;
W.Wharton

NOTABLE HORSES:
French Beige; Rowston Manor; Calpurnius; Waterloo; Abbeydale;
Mountain Cross; Teleprompter; Kazoo; Colway Bold; Satank.

OWNERS:
Sheikh Mohammed; Lord Derby; Lord Swaythling;
Duke Of Sutherland; Mrs M.Haggas;
Mr R. Coleman; Joe L. Allbritton; R.Sangster;
James Westoll; A.K.Collins; Gerald Cooper;
Kirk Bloodstock; Mrs Susan Rudolf; Mrs.M.Irwin

National Hunt & Dual Purpose Stables

Whitcombe Manor, Dorset.

Peter Bolton

Most racing stables grow in stages as the requirements of their occupants change. More often than not, the only governing principle in the design of new stabling, apart from the perennial desire to cut costs, is a vague adherence to tradition. Whitcombe Manor, the most significant new yard to be built in Britain since Sam Darling built Warren Place in the late 1920s, has changed all that.

Five years ago, the land on which Whitcombe Manor now stands was a greenfield site, half a mile from the tiny hamlet of Whitcombe, which itself is situated a few miles south east of Dorchester. It is the brainchild of a deceptively softly spoken, Dorset-born businessman called Peter Bolton, who, in his own words, wanted "to create a centre of excellence where the care of the horse was paramount".

Bolton is not an iconoclast - he professes himself to be a great fan of the traditional side of the game - but neither is he scared to criticise racing's structure and the attitudes of many people in the sport. "Having had horses in training for many years with various companies of mine, racing's shortcomings were very obvious to me and I suspect to a lot of other people who come to it from other walks of life. No names, no pack drill but I felt that in terms of communication between owner and trainer and in the care of the horses, a lot was lacking".

Whitcombe's creator, Peter Bolton.

The design of the racing stables at Whitcombe was an attempt to address one side of the equation; the care of the horse. Bolton describes the design as "a mixture of old and new". As well as visiting perhaps the best example of traditional stable design in the country at Kingsclere, Bolton sought the latest scientific advice from academics on both sides of the Atlantic. From Professor Andrew Clark of the Equine Science Department of Ontario State University, Bolton derived an advanced failsafe ventilation system. "Each of the boxes, which are all insulated, is 14ft by 14ft and above the door is a ventilator, which is matched by a little dormer vent at the back. The theory being that in the unlikely event of shutting a

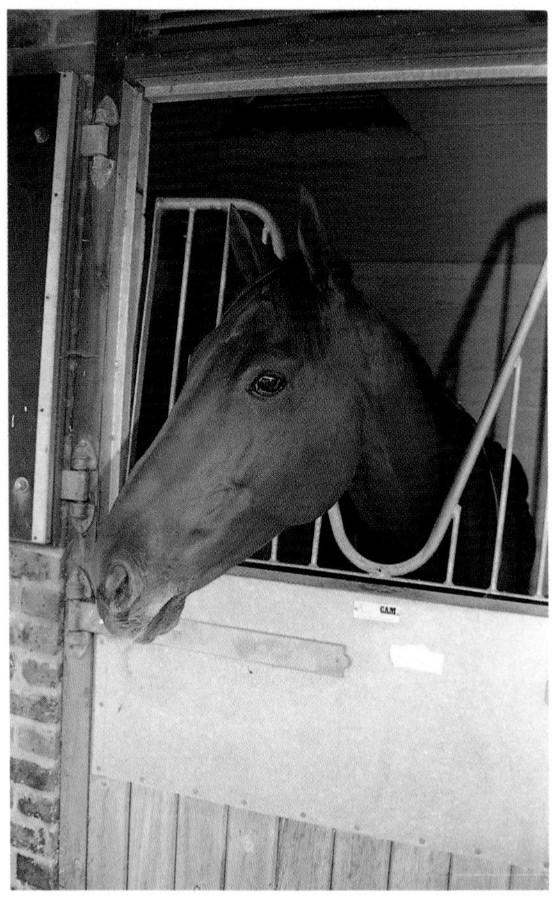

Gold Cup winners deserve the best. Cool Ground and luxury pad.

top door, you would still get sufficient movement of air from the body heat of the horse. The air comes in through the mid vent and out again, taking airborne spores away".

Stable staff also benefit from Whitcombe's carefully thought out design. A massive, cantilevered overhang above the stable door protects the stable lad, as well as the horse itself, from the elements, without the danger of injury that could result from extra upright members.

Such unusually painstaking attention to detail is the lynchpin of Bolton's philosophy: "People who can afford to own racehorses are usually successful in what they are doing and are probably going to be quite fastidious about the care of their investments. I wanted to create a place where that was possible". In the event of accident or illness, Whitcombe also has an on-site vet in the shape of Brian Eagles, past President of the Equine Veterinary Society, who was formerly with Guy Harwood for nine years at Pulborough.

The intensely insular racing world has traditionally viewed "outsiders" with suspicion, particularly those with new ideas and Bolton's innovations have proved no exception. The management structure at Whitcombe has also proved hard for racing traditionalists to grasp. Most wealthy patrons of the past have remained at one step removed from the day to day business of the yard. Peter Bolton, by contrast, has an office on site, next door to the offices of his trainers and delights in being close to the action.

The return of Reg Akehurst to his South Hatch stables at Epsom after finding himself unable to settle at Whitcombe was cited as proof by hidebound doubters that "good facilities aren't everything". The blow of losing Akehurst, who complained of not being able to settle in Dorset and of missing Epsom, was softened by the arrival of one of the few dual purpose trainers of equivalent stature, Toby Balding, who arrived at Whitcombe on a short term basis. Ironically, the new partnership's greatest success in their relatively short time together has come with Cool Ground, a horse trained originally, of course, by Reg Akehurst. Cool Ground's thrilling victory in the Gold Cup under a stirring ride from the precociously brilliant Adrian Maguire has, however, failed to cement the relationship between Balding and Bolton. The former Weyhill trainer is still anxious to get back to his roots and is building a new yard on the Hampshire Downs, close to his former base.

In the meantime, Balding has been joined at Whitcombe by yet another top dual purpose trainer in the shape of David Elsworth (arguably the only 'mixed' trainer of appropriate stature who has not yet trained from Whitcombe) whose former training business has been taken over

One of the finest all weather gallops in the country, according to Toby Balding. Gone Savage and Regal Scintilla take advantage.

Work rider, Clive Bailey.

by Peter Bolton, and who is now operating between his old yard at Whitsbury and Whitcombe. For Bolton, the acquisition of David Elsworth's business was a very shrewd move. Not only has he secured the services of one of the country's most able trainers but he has also gained access to the famous old grass gallops at Whitsbury. He is understandably delighted: "By combining these two centres, we have absolutely the best combined facilities in the country. By having the use of what must be among the finest and oldest gallops in the country, we have completed the last piece in the jigsaw". With characteristic foresight, Bolton was well prepared for the possibility of Whitcombe being shared. There are five self-contained yards within the overall complex, catering for just about every economic eventuality. The division of the yard into two separate entities has posed no problems at all.

Whatever form training takes in the future at Whitcombe Manor, there is no doubt that it is a significant and impressive venture. Peter Bolton has already begun to achieve the results that his efforts deserve. The main stumbling block in the way of future success, however, is Whitcombe's geographical isolation from the majority of racecourses and the inadequacy of the road network. If racing were centralised and Peter Bolton's Dorchester racecourse had been granted planning permission as one of those centres, Whitcombe Manor's future would have been assured. Trainers would have been clamouring at the door to get the chance of using its facilities. As things stand, Whitcombe's future seems dependent on keeping the services of top class dual purpose trainers, of which there is a finite, and fast diminishing, supply.

PROPRIETOR:
Peter Bolton

TRAINERS:
Toby Balding; David Elsworth

PAST TRAINERS:
Richard Mitchell; Reg Akehurst

OWNERS:
Duke of Atholl; Lord Chetwode; R.J. Lavelle; Miss B. Swire; Tony Geake; Michael Jackson Bloodstock Ltd; Michael Kerr-Dineen; Jack Maxwell; Whitcombe Manor Racing Stables Ltd; Colin Buckle; J.M. Beeby; Ernest Weinstein; Heather Bare; K.L. Perrin; Sydney Mason.

NOTABLE HORSES:
Regal Scintilla; Cool Ground

Uplands, Upper Lambourn.

Charlie Brooks

Uplands is indivisibly associated in the memory of most jumping people with one man: Fred Winter. The tough and universally respected Winter is one of the few champion jockeys to have carved out a fresh and equally successful career as a trainer. He transformed Uplands, a relatively anonymous corner of the racing hamlet of Upper Lambourn, turning it into one of the landmarks of the National Hunt scene with the exploits of great horses like Bula, Crisp, Pendil, Midnight Court and Lanzarote.

The yard has not just been a prolific source of equine talent; a significant proportion of the leading figures involved in National Hunt racing today have, at one time or another, passed through the Uplands academy. In addition to Winter's successor at Uplands, Charlie Brooks, top National Hunt trainers Nicky Henderson, Oliver Sherwood, the "greatest jockey", John Francome and Sheikh Mohammed's racing manager, Anthony Stroud all served their racing apprenticeship at the yard.

Uplands' fame in the jumping world is a relatively recent phenomenon. Prior to Winter's arrival in the summer of 1964, it was known, primarily, as a source of good flat handicappers, under the shrewd tutelage of Charlie Pratt, brother of Freddie Pratt who, for half a century, was private trainer to James de Rothschild at the Lambourn stable, Lethornes (there, he

Brian Delaney, head lad at Uplands since Fred Winter's day, leads the string on the public gallops.

All Jeff gets a scrub down in front of the boxes known as 'Millionaire's Row'.

enjoyed the special privilege of a roped-off private gallop on the otherwise public gallops at Mandown). Younger brother, Charlie, was a former head lad to Harry Cottrill and never had many more than twenty horses in at any one time, but, nevertheless achieved a number of notable successes in the top handicaps. Tragically, he was killed in a plane crash returning from the scene of one of his best wins, in a valuable handicap at Redcar.

For the best part of eighteen months, Uplands lay empty. It had been bought at auction by the doyen of current Lambourn trainers, Doug Marks, who now trains at Freddie Pratt's old yard, Lethornes but its new owner had second thoughts about his purchase and never moved in. At the time of the auction, Fred Winter, along with his wife, Diana, had eyed the property with great interest but was committed to another season of race riding. Luckily, Doug Marks was a close friend and, after hearing that Uplands' new owner had yet to move in, the Winters made a private offer, which was accepted.

When Fred Winter first moved into the yard, in the summer of 1964, it was a mess but, characteristically, Uplands' new guvnor could see that, underneath the weeds and the broken glass, lay a potentially top class training establishment. After all, just next door, on a similarly sized plot of land, was one of the most successful jumping yards of the time, Saxon House, the source of Fred Winter's great Gold Cup triumph on Mandarin, and from where, only a few months earlier, Fulke Walwyn had sent out the great Team Spirit, to win the Grand National. Incredibly, the very next year, Winter's fledgling team trumped the exploits of "over the wall", as the lads nicknamed Saxon House, with the performance of the American horse, Jay Trump, in the 1965 Grand National.

The rest is jumping history: after winning the National again the next year with Anglo, Winter went on to collect just about every top prize in the calendar and established Uplands as the leading National Hunt yard of its day. It is an unlikely setting for such honours. Although Fred Winter expanded Uplands' capacity to sixty boxes, in comparison with the great training establishments of the flat there is nothing which sets the yard apart from the ordinary (apart, that is, from that intangible atmosphere, which comes from association with great sporting success). Like all the other yards in Upper Lambourn, there is very little space for manoeuvre and few private facilities.

Charlie Brooks, the young man saddled with the unenviable task of following in Fred Winter's footsteps, agrees: "Your movements are dictated by the surroundings and we've got limitations here, in that the only land we have is a small paddock, but we're very close to the gallops and schooling grounds, which are very good". At present, there are rather more empty boxes than Brooks would like. "Ideally, I'd like a team of about eighty. 100 would be too many, but the more material you have, the more chance of success".

Fred Winter's successor has inherited more than just the yard from his former boss, in the shape of a knowledgeable and loyal staff, whose help Brooks has found invaluable. Brian Delaney, Fred Winter's head lad for many years, who has been at Uplands since the early days in 1964, is still "the sergeant major" and many of the lads have stayed on with the new guv'nor. Since taking over, Brooks has found that he enjoys training more than he ever imagined. "For a long time, I had no intention of taking up training but when the opportunity arose, I thought it was too good an opportunity to miss, so I grabbed the chance. Since then, I've become much more committed to the horses. When I first came to Mr Winter, I was keen on racing but not so interested in what went on in the yard. Now, the reverse is true. I'm indifferent to standing around in racecourse bars, having conversations with drunks who promise you horses, but very enthusiastic about training and developing the horses themselves, although I still don't relish walking around smelling of horses all the time".

A well earned rest after the morning's exertions.

Far from being a dilletante Old Etonian afraid of getting his hands dirty, Brooks is very much a hands-on trainer around the yard, which he is anxious to develop. Much of the 1992 close season was spent overseeing the construction of a new loose school. "Now, for the first time, we can loose school at home. It's important to try and think of ways to develop and improve".

For Brooks, inheriting the Winter preserve has been a mixed blessing. As well as the useful contacts and the high profile have come the inevitable but unwelcome

Sadly, in recession-hit Upper Lambourn, full boxes are the exception rather than the rule.

comparisons. "I think that, being relatively young, some owners deal with you in a way that they would never have dealt with Fred Winter but you have to take the rough with the smooth".

PAST TRAINERS:
Charlie Pratt; Fred Winter

PAST ASSISTANTS:
Nicky Henderson; Anthony Stroud; Oliver Sherwood; Charlie Brooks

NOTABLE HORSES:
Jay Trump; Anglo; Crisp; Pendil; Rough and Tumble; Midnight Court; Bula; Lanzarote; Fifty Dollars More; Half Free; Plundering; Celtic Shot

OWNERS:
Lady Joseph; Nigel Dempster; Vice Admiral Sir Fitzroy Talbot; Lord Crawshaw; Gerard Nock; John Halliday; Mrs Richard Stanley; Jim McCarthy; R.E.A. Bott (Wigmore St) Ltd; C.F. van Straubenzee; Paul Green; Mrs G.Rowan-Hamilton; G.F. Beddington; Mrs B. Mead; Ali Saeed; Miss M.Talbot; Mrs G. Abecassis; Peter Spicer; Mrs W. Tulloch; D.E.H. Horton; Mrs Gary Black; N.H. Gardner; Miss M. Felstead; R.A.B. Whittle; Mrs M.J. Cobham; Mrs Basil Samuel

HORSE TO FOLLOW:
Le Ginno

Kinnersley, Worcestershire.

Simon Christian

The Rimell family association with the picturesque Worcestershire yard of Kinnersley is one of the longest of its kind in National Hunt racing, stretching back well over half a century, and even though Mercy Rimell has now relinquished the licence and retired to nearby Upton, the connection is not entirely severed. Fred and Mercy Rimell's grandson, Mark, become the fourth generation of the family to be associated with the yard in his role as assistant to the new boss, Simon Christian - Fulke Walwyn's former assistant - who took over the yard in 1989.

Finding a successor to the Rimell dynasty must have been quite a task for Kinnersley's landlords, the Croome Estate, formerly the property of the Earls of Coventry but now part of the insurance company, Sun Alliance's land holdings. There would be no shortage of applicants for what must surely be one of the most enviable positions in jump racing but at the same time, finding the right person to follow in the Rimells' illustrious footsteps must have been difficult.

Simon Christian was one of a number of enthusiastic hopefuls queueing up for the chance to train from such a hallowed yard. "I'd heard a rumour that a Lambourn trainer might be moving there and a friend said why didn't I try? At the time, I was renting two small yards in Lambourn, which were some distance apart. There were no paddocks and no staff accommodation, so the attractions of a self-contained place like Kinnersley, with its own land, were obvious".

Walking to work against a backdrop of the Malverns.

Christian's first impressions of the famous old yard, a place he had read and heard a lot about but never seen, were not entirely favourable. "To be honest, I was a bit disappointed by my first glimpse because, as you come off the A38, the yard is not seen to best effect, with the outside boxes and modern barn to the fore. But as soon as I walked into the main yard with the lime trees, where all those famous horses had been stood up, and later when I saw the fields and gallops, I was enchanted by the place".

To anyone with first hand experience of Kinnersley, this will come as no surprise; its

'The all weather', a necessity on Kinnersley's clay soil.

250 acres of gallops and paddocks are among the most varied and interesting in the country. Quite apart from its track record for producing top class chasers and the stunning views of the Malverns in the middle distance, Kinnersley boasts unexpected extras such as a private cricket pitch (a real bonus for a cricket fan like Simon Christian) and a collection of stunning, Robert Adam-designed, garden buildings and follies dotted around the estate.

The yard itself was built around the turn of the century by the Earl Of Coventry for his son, Charlie Coventry, who became Kinnersley's first trainer. Earlier that century, the Ninth Earl had sent out the winners of two successive Grand Nationals in Emblem and Emblematic from his own private stables. It is a pleasantly detailed, traditional yard that bears the slightly regimented look of much estate building, with its neat brickwork and regular casement windows. The main quadrangle is lined with lime trees, severely cut back in past times but now allowed to grow more freely. When Simon Christian took over the yard, the estate took the opportunity to refurbish the facilities. Although the main interiors were almost completely gutted, the restoration has been sensitive and in keeping, with all the original features maintained. Now the tack rooms, vets' room, drying rooms and laundry are on the ground floor of the main building, with a twelve bedroom hostel above.

Even though Kinnersley was a power in the land throughout the Rimell years - Fred Rimell topping the trainers' lists several times - its capacity has never been greater than 40 boxes. In the 1930s, Tom Rimell had around 35 horses, a figure that remained roughly the norm, even

Robert Adam's Panorama, centrepiece of Kinnersley's picturesque parkland.

during his son's most successful years. Simon Christian was surprised to find how small the yard was. "I think a lot of people expect a famous yard like Kinnersley to have a large capacity and it was certainly smaller than I had imagined but Mr Walwyn once said to me that you "only need 40 to go to war jumping'."

For 1992-93, the Christian 'army' numbered around 30, of which a dozen are three and four year old novices. This is a creditable step-up in recessionary times from the 1991-92 season. "We only ran 23 last year and never had more than 25 in". Christian is a traditionalist by inclination, and it is clear from his buying policy (a trio of lovely looking Strong Gales troop out for third lot as we speak) and from what he says about the preparation of chasers, that Fulke Walwyn was a great influence on the fledgling horseman. "I often think what might he have done in a given situation. One thing I particularly used to respect was his ability to see a horse's potential very quickly and he'd get them fit but not at the expense of their long term well being. Horses like Crimson Embers and Diamond Edge would not have been the champions they were without delicate preparations".

The rolling hills of Kinnersley are even better suited to such preparations than the Lambourn gallops used by Fulke Walwyn. Apart from the M5, which cuts the property in two and is crossed by means of a bridge, the horses can walk and trot for miles uninterrupted around the steep banks and rolling hills of the estate. The clay soil of Worcestershire is very different from the chalk downland of Berkshire and Simon Christian has had to adapt his training methods

Kinnersley's first post-Rimell guv'nor, Simon Christian.

accordingly. "The ground here can get much worse than on the downs and the all weather strip, which is wide enough to get three upsides, is essential".

Adaptation has been made easier by the helpful advice of the former first lady of Kinnersley, Mercy Rimell, who is still a regular visitor at the yard and has a horse in training with her successor, 'done' by her grandson Mark. "They used to gallop them more in the old days. My father-in-law, Tom Rimell, in particular did a lot more work. The great joy of Kinnersley is that, with the hills and all the land there's no need to go on the roads. It's easy to keep horses sweet in a place like this".

PAST TRAINERS:
Hon. Charles Coventry; Ben Roberts; Tom Rimell; Fred Rimell

PAST ASSISTANTS:
Kim Bailey; Michael Bell

NOTABLE HORSES:
Emblem; Emblematic (trained at Kinnersley in nineteenth century but not from present yard); Forbra; E.S.B; Nicolaus Silver; Gay Trip; Rag Trade; Woodland Venture; Royal Frolic; Comedy of Errors; Gaye Brief.

OWNERS:
Brigadier A.H. Parker Bowles; M.D.W .Wilson; Paul Morris; Allan Lamb/Ginny Leng Racing plc; P. Curling; Mrs John Hughes; Mrs Valerie Lewis; Lynn Wilson; N. Robinson; Z.S. Clark; Mrs B. Whitehouse; J.R. Holmes; Mrs Adrian Ireland; P.J. Doherty; C.A. McMillan; Mr Donnelly White.

HORSE TO FOLLOW:
Lost Buccaneer

Danebury, Stockbridge.

Ken Cunningham-Brown

The Andover to Redbridge branch of the London and South Western Railway once rattled with horse traffic travelling from Stockbridge to the racecourses of England and beyond. Hard though it may be to believe, now that virtually all traces have been covered over, but Stockbridge was once one of the most populous training centres in the country.

The focus of all this activity was the town's racecourse. Stockbridge racecourse is, of course, long since defunct (the last meeting was in 1898) but its track, still overlooked by the ruin of its once distinguished grandstand, survives to provide a picturesque gallop for another historic relic of the town's past, namely the Danebury training establishment, revived after forty fallow years by dual-purpose trainer, Ken Cunningham-Brown.

For turf historians, this is welcome news. In the nineteenth century, Danebury and its near neighbour Chattis Hill (now largely built over) were names to conjure with in racing circles, on a par with, say, Warren Place and Manton. Witness the reverential tone adopted by a Victorian racing writer on the occasion of a visit to Danebury: "What a silent deserted road is that we traverse, and in the mysterious stillness of the downs exists a charm not to be described. In such a solitude, sight of the white rails of the racecourse is almost startling, and then we pass near the stands from which the cream of British sportsmen have witnessed many a contest

The big house at Danebury still stands, next door to the new yard, but is no longer connected with racing.

Ken Cuningham-Brown feeds the yearlings in the depths of midwinter.

destined to live in turf history. Next comes a turn to the right, and lo! Danebury is before us".

Danebury today has changed a great deal. The imposing house survives intact, as does its forerunner, the much more modest cottage that was the original home of John Barham Day, but it no longer forms part of the Danebury training establishment. When Ken Cunningham-Brown bought the estate, he decided that the priority was to restore the gallops, so the house was sold off.

The purchase of the estate had been fraught with problems. "We'd moved to the area for business and I got to know Vernon Cross, who was the last person to train at Chattis Hill before the gallops were ploughed up. I had one or two horses with him and when I decided that I wanted to train, he took me on as a sort of amateur student to show me the ropes. When I eventually started looking around for somewhere to train, I heard about the gallops at Danebury. The owners were a pair of elderly brothers, who were very hard to deal with. One of today's leading trainers came up to look at the old place and was shot at! Eventually, however, we managed to buy the place. The old stables were totally ruinous but the gallops had only been grazed by sheep and so were in reasonable shape".

The modern face of training at Stockbridge.

After much consultation of old maps, Cunningham-Brown was able to trace the course of the old gallops and, after much careful nurture, bring them back into use. Some of these marvellous downland turf gallops have been in use since the beginning of the nineteenth century and perhaps longer and have certainly never been ploughed up in living memory. The most famous of these is the Danebury Hill gallop, four furlongs round, followed by a stiff six furlong climb, starting gradually and finishing up with a very steep last furlong. John Day was notoriously severe with his horses, once replying to a friend who questioned the logic of testing a delicate horse on Danebury Hill, "I like to know the worst as well as the best".

There are now 300 acres devoted entirely to training at the revamped Danebury, consisting of gallops, schooling ground, woods and paddocks. Cunningham-Brown's small string must be among the most privileged in training, a fact that is beginning to be

The old Stockbridge racecourse (above) provides the scene for the present day gallops. The ivy-covered ruins of the old Stockbridge grandstand can still be seen (right).

reflected in results. "Last year (1990-91) we only had 15 horses but we had 15 winners on the flat and if you'd had £1 to win on every horse, you would be £136 up, which must be some sort of record!". Cunningham-Brown believes that individual attention and relaxation are the keys to improved performance. "I feed them personally every day and there's a food chemist in the Unichem Group (of which Cunningham-Brown is now a non-executive director) who helps me with any problems. The other crucial thing is for a horse to be contented mentally and in a place like this, it is easy to switch horses off and make them relax. There are any number of woodland walks and changes of scenery to freshen them up".

The racing world has traditionally looked askance on those 'amateurs' who turn to racing as a hobby, a fact that irritates successful businessman turned trainer, Ken Cunningham-Brown: "I think people ought to be judged according to their results. I'm tired of being known as that businessman who trains horses. As far as I'm concerned I'm a horseman that trains horses. For the past few seasons, I've had nothing but horses with bad legs and horses with problems and I think I've shown that I can improve them".

Danebury stalwart, Modesto.

The new Danebury's ever-increasing string is the best testament to Cunningham-Brown's skills as a trainer. A new traditional yard is planned to complement the existing American-style barn and accommodate thirty more horses. "We're rattling around at the moment. There's no reason, with the facilities that we have at Danebury, why 100 horses couldn't be trained here". It might be a bit over-optimistic to talk of reviving the glory days of John Day just yet but, thanks to the sterling efforts of an ex-businessman, who has proved himself very much a horseman, a precious part of racing's heritage is back on the map.

PAST TRAINERS:
John Barham Day; John Day Junior; Tom Cannon Sen & Jun; Fred Withington; H.T Young; P.W. Collins

PAST ASSISTANTS:
Mick Channon

NOTABLE HORSES:
Bay Middleton; Crucifix; Chateau d'Espagne; Grey Momus; The Ugly Buck; Mendicant; Pyrrhus the First; The Hermit; Andover; Vauban; Siberia; Scottish Queen; Repulse; Cossack; Mincepie; Busybody

OWNERS:
A.J. Richards; D. Bass; M.D. Brunton; David Gower; Trevor Mitchell; Fiona Brunton; Miss Julie Self; Roy Cornish; G.J. Cronin; M. Green; D.M. Madden; Jerry Bugden; Mrs F. Jackman; J. Chapman; S. Black; B. Short; S. Peterson; James Hickman; Harry Rednapp; By Chance Racing; Mrs Reid; Mrs Emery; R. Sears

Clear Height Stables, Epsom.

Simon Dow

Once a year, the world's sporting media descends on Derby Stables Road, the home of Simon Dow's Clear Height Stables, and ignores the latter completely.

For most of the dozen or so trainers who make up Epsom's tightly-knit little racing community, Derby Day is not so much about racing (leave that to the Maktoum family and Robert Sangster) as public relations. It is a time for reflected glory and the provision of seductive perks for the loyal band of owners who keep Epsom in business as a training centre. Unlike the hoi polloi, who, on Derby Day, struggle to park and to find somewhere to drink, this is the day when an Epsom owner can swank right up to the Downs, roll into his private paddock and spend the day feeling superior in one of the private marquees that Epsom trainers, almost without exception, erect on their land for the big day.

No set of owners has it easier than Simon Dow's. Clear Height is right slap bang in the middle of the action: within spitting distance of the grandstand, and right next door to the Derby Stables. For most of the year, Simon Dow, like any other keen young trainer, spends much of his time persuading people through the gates. On Derby Day, he has to employ security guards to keep them out.

Clear Height Stables came into being in 1957, the year that Lester Piggott won his second Derby, on Crepello (such is racing's continuity that, on the occasion of my visit to the yard, thirty five years later minus one day, Lester was riding a winner for the stable at Folkestone). The man responsible for transforming Clear Height from a bare field into one of the area's most successful yards is Epsom's eminence grise, Ron Smyth, who retired from training in 1991, after forty four seasons of crafty handicap placements and hard graft, and still lives in the house he built next door.

Simon Dow and Gallant Effort.

Smyth's family have been to Epsom what the Jarvis dynasty is to Newmarket. At one time, just after the Second World War, no less than five members of the family trained at Epsom, the most prominent of whom, Ron Smyth's father, Herbert 'the guv'nor' Smyth, trained from a yard right opposite the grandstand, next door to the Derby Arms pub.

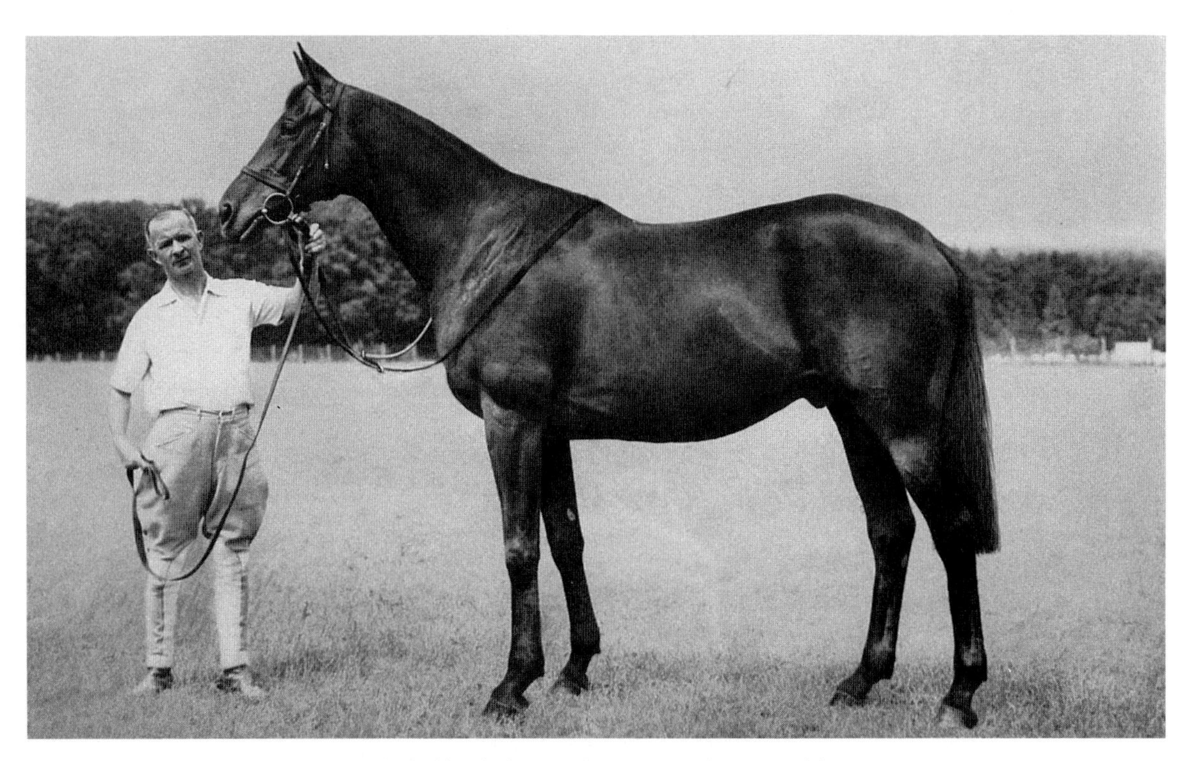

'The builder of Clear Height', Ron Smyth's Harrowful.

The money to build Clear Height Stables came, according to the wily old trainer himself, from a number of successful betting coups on a horse called Harrowful, who Smyth describes as "the builder of Clear Height". "We bought him for £130 and, in my betting days, I can hardly ever remember him letting us down". The old horse lived on at the stable he helped to build until he was thirty two years old.

From his new purpose-built fifty box yard, the former champion National Hunt jockey was a formidable adversary under both sets of rules as a trainer, winning numerous top flat race handicaps as well as twice sending out the winner of the Triumph Hurdle. Although he had decent horses like Combermore, who was second in the Irish Derby and won at Royal Ascot, Smyth's forte (just like his former apprentice, Geoff Lewis, today) was preparing horses for the big handicaps. The prolific Tremblant and Flash Imp are the two he recalls with greatest fondness.

Smyth's successor and tenant, Simon Dow, gains the shrewd old handler's no nonsense seal of approval. "He's a hard working fella who knows his job". This is a view shared by most people in the industry, who have nothing but admiration for the way in which this serious and applied young man (30 years of age but looks ten years younger) squeezes the best out of the largely moderate raw material at his disposal. It is no surprise to see that he has been deservedly rewarded, in these recessionary times, with a healthy string of forty horses.

Although relatively new to training, Dow is no newcomer to Epsom. Although not connected with racing in any way, he was "hooked on horses" from an early age, mucking out in Michael Haynes' then livery stable at thirteen years old and then joining the yard full-time when he left school eight years later when Haynes took out a training licence. He has been at Epsom ever since, apart from a spell running his own livery yard, working himself up via an assistant's job with Philip Mitchell.

"There is no horse that you couldn't train at Epsom. They used to say that you couldn't train long distance hurdlers and chasers here until Reg (Akehurst) proved them wrong and there is no reason why classic horses cannot be trained here". (The next day, Silver Wisp's excellent third in the Derby provided ample corroboration of this statement).

Dow concedes, however, that there is an Epsom type: "The training grounds are on the camber, like the racecourse itself and short legged, quick actioned horses tend to work best here. Any horse can work aerobically here but, I suppose there might be occasions, if you wanted to do a Jack Berry and make them forward by giving them experience and to get them spot on first time out, you might conceivably want to take them to a racecourse. Epsom-trained horses tend to do well at Brighton and Goodwood".

Simon Dow leads the string in taking a turn in front of the empty Epsom grandstands.

Bucking the trend, Clear Heights is full to capacity.

Watching second lot picking their way past the noise and bustle of the Downs the day before Dr Devious' Derby, calmly negotiating traffic and gypsy caravans alike, Dow comments that "our two year olds experience as much life here as four year olds elsewhere. They learn quickly not to get worried by anything". The current apple of Dow's eye, Born to Be, a robust filly by Never So Bold, passes by, looking head and shoulders above her mostly plating class companions. "I wish I had a few more like that one. Her owner, Mr Redmond, just walked into the yard one day and said, 'if you break these two yearlings for me, I'll send you a useless filly. I agreed, did the job and he sent me this one, which won first time out. I wish training was always that easy'."

What makes Dow's current level of success admirable is that he has gained entry to the charmed circle of racehorse trainers without the backing of long-established money, patronage or racing pedigree. It was particularly rotten luck that Khalid Abdulla chose to remove his horses from the yard on Ron Smyth's retirement; perhaps after a season or two more of Dow showing what his skills can accomplish, the Prince might be tempted to resume his patronage.

PAST TRAINERS:
Ron Smyth

NOTABLE HORSES:
Tremblant; Heaven Knows; Combermore; Flash Imp; Harrowful; Blarney Beacon; Boxer

OWNERS:
J. Redmond; Mrs G.R. Smith; C.F. Sparrowhawk; M.F. Kentish; Ray Hawthorn; Mrs A.M. Hill; K. Butler; John.A. Kelly; Mrs Redmond; Ralph Cross; S.A. Walker; P. Chakko and Mrs Heather Chakko; Mrs S.R. Crowe; Mrs G. Jarvis; Roger Sayer; Rogan Langton; T.R. Pearson; R.A.S. Castle; Beaufort Bloodstock; Gravy Boys Racing; Eurostrait Ltd; Visual Identity Ltd; Under Orders Syndicate; Sunset and Vine plc; Geoffrey Bishop

HORSE TO FOLLOW:
Young Ern

Habton Grange, Malton.

Peter Easterby

The Easterby family home at Great Habton, near Malton in North Yorkshire, has deep associations with the turf, but it is only in the present generation that it has become a fully-fledged training establishment. The area around Habton, to the north of Malton, is flat, fertile farming country, very different in character from the main Malton work grounds south of the town and, for many years, arable crops, rather than horseflesh, have been its mainstay. Even today, trucks, heavily laden with potatoes, compete with horse traffic on the narrow roads round about, and on the fields surrounding Habton Grange, all weather and turf gallops coincide neatly with the furrows of the plough.

After no less than forty two years of training throughout the year, non-stop, on the flat and over the jumps, Peter Easterby shows no sign of slacking. His rambling, rabbit warren of a yard, which has expanded over the years to accommodate ever-burgeoning numbers, is as full to bursting as ever and the winners continue to roll in, seemingly regardless of the season. Asking M.H. Easterby about giving up training is as pointless as asking L. Piggott about hanging up his boots, and the answer is much the same. "Why should you give up doing something you enjoy? Anyway, what else would I do?".

Peter Easterby first took out a licence to train at Habton Grange, or Habton Stud as it was then known, in 1950. Before that, the premises had been used as a farm for a number of years, although there were always horses around. "My father used to deal in a few horses from here, but it was a farm mainly". Even today, the yard retains the homely atmosphere of a family farm.

Gallops combine with ploughed fields on the flat fertile farmland at Habton.

Everything is spick and span, but rather than the formality of neat courtyards, most of the boxes seem to have sprung up, in typically utilitarian Yorkshire fashion, as and when they were needed. A number have been converted from existing farm buildings and a large hay barn serves as a makeshift covered ride.

Although it had never formally been a racing yard, the farm at Great Habton had been used for a number of years by the then Highfield House trainer, H.D. Bazley, as an overspill yard and before that had been the family home of that famous Yorkshire training dynasty, the Collings. Both R.J. and George Colling were born at Great Habton, where their father, the jockey and trainer R.W. Colling, had farmed for a number of years at the turn of the century.

The young Peter Easterby had long entertained notions of being a trainer and, as a teenager, worked "as a muggins" for that great Irish horseman, Frank Hartigan at Weyhill, an experience that left a mark, in more ways than one. "He was a great trainer but a very bad tempered man - he didn't care if he hit you with a fork or a rake". After returning from two years National Service with the Royal Veterinary Corps at Melton Mowbray, a training career beckoned. "It was the only way I could think of to earn a living". Soon after the twenty year old Easterby took out a licence, the vagaries of the training business were brought home to him by the death of his old boss, Frank Hartigan. "He was a great trainer but a bad businessman, and died skint".

Such a fate is unlikely to befall Peter Easterby, who, in addition to his renown as a trainer, has long enjoyed a reputation for shrewdness in his buying and selling of horses. Bearing in mind the sheer number of horses that must have passed though his hands over the years, his powers of recall are extraordinary. Looking at his entry in a 1955 copy of *Horses in Training*, the veteran trainer not only remembers the racing career of every one of the 12 strong string, but also how much they cost and how much he sold them for. The list, accompanied by the Easterby commentary, is typical, in its variety, of the mixed yard that Habton Grange has always been. There was Double Rose, "the yard's first winner, at Market Rasen"; Ohms Law: "a good chaser, third in the Foxhunters"; Welburn Hill: "sold him for six grand, which was quite a bit of money in them days" and King's Coup: "first good flat horse we had, picked him up for 720 guineas" and so on.

No close season for the workaholic Peter Easterby.

Although Peter Easterby has made certain races 'his own', most notably the Champion Hurdle, during his long and distinguished career, he has never specialised in a particular kind of horse. His only philosophy is "to buy sound horses. If you don't get that right, you've got no chance". Easterby plainly gets as much pleasure training a top class sprint handicapper like Cumbrian Waltzer as he does a promising young novice chaser, such as Young Benz. Even during the glory years of Sea Pigeon and Night Nurse when, for an incredible six consecutive years, an Easterby

The late Lady Murless' St Ninian now combines racing with stud duties.

horse finished in the first two in the Champion Hurdle, Great Habton continued to send out a stream of good winners on the flat. In recent years, Peter Easterby has tended back towards the flat, topping the list of Yorkshire trainers more often than not and helping long serving stable jockey, Mark Birch, to the "Cock o'the North" jockey's title on a number of occasions.

Unlike many "oldtimers", who retreat into tales of the good old days, the ever versatile Peter Easterby is far too busy, even at the fag end of a long flat season, to think about the past. When pushed, he will admit that "you can't win with low grade horses like you used to" but with five runners that afternoon in a top class jumping programme at Wetherby to occupy the mind, low grade horses are not really M.H. Easterby's concern any more.

PAST TRAINERS:
R.W. Colling; R.J. Colling; H.D. Bazley; W. Easterby
(all of the above lived at Habton but none trained actively from it)

NOTABLE HORSES:
Bronze Hill; Goldhill; Saucy Kit; Night Nurse; Sea Pigeon; Little Owl; St.Ninian; Cumbrian Waltzer; Young Benz

OWNERS:
Sir Neil Westbrook; P.D. Savill; Maj J.S. Linley; Paul Green; T. Dyer; G.E. Shouler; Cumbrian Industrials; W. Pratt; Peter Hurst; Gymcrak Thoroughbred Racing; T.D. Easterby; Mrs I. Bray; N.A. Ryall; Jennifer Pallister; Miss.E. Macregor; Fred Wilson; P.A. Sullivan; Peter Bourke; F.C. Ballard; Ian Armitage; B. Shaw; I. Bell; Mrs S.J. Mason; Mrs S. Johnstone; T.H. Bennett; A.M. Wragg; Mrs J.B. Mountifield; G.H. Leatham; Mrs Anne Henson; Mrs S.D. Murray; Jonathan Gill; W. Pratt; A. Watson.

HORSE TO FOLLOW:
Bollin Magdelene

WHITSBURY.

DAVID ELSWORTH

N THE CHURCHYARD above the small Hampshire village of Whitsbury is a familiar name in an unfamiliar setting. Inscribed on a modest headstone in a quiet corner of the graveyard is a name more usually seen emblazoned on the garish fascia boards of a thousand betting shops across the country: William Hill.

In death as in life, he is surrounded by the indirect source of his wealth, racehorses. The graveyard is bordered by the paddocks of his beloved stud and within sight of the grave, mares pick grass attended by their foals. It is a picturesque rural scene, a lifetime's hard work away from the cheap ring at the White City, where the tough brummie runaway first made his mark. Hill's rise to pre-eminence in the rough world of the betting ring in the 1930s was meteoric. In twenty years, he had graduated from the silver ring to the rails and made enough money by the age of 40 to purchase the Whitsbury estate, near Fordingbridge in Hampshire.

William Hill's grave in the Whitsbury churchyard.

The main yard at Whitsbury has contained racehorses since at least the latter part of the nineteenth century and possibly before that but prior to William Hill's involvement, Whitsbury had rarely hit the headlines. There was only one racing yard on the estate, containing about thirty decrepit, lapboarded boxes with a leaking corrugated iron roof. The estate was the property of Sir Charles Hyde, the then proprietor of the *Birmingham Post* newspaper, whose private trainer, Norman Scobie, did his best with a small string of moderate flat horses.

William Hill's main objective at Whitsbury was to develop the stud, which still runs successfully today, but the owning of racehorses always exercised an appeal for the great bookmaker. Monty Smyth was his first private trainer at Whitsbury for many years, before 'going public' in 1958. Most of the success that Hill achieved on the racecourse, however, came from horses trained elsewhere, with Henry Count at Chantilly, Captain Charles Elsey at Malton and Bruce Hobbs at Newmarket.

In the early 1960s, Hill decided that

Whitsbury's famous head lad, Rodney Boult,
Desert Orchid's racecourse jinx.

Whitsbury would become a major force as a training establishment and set about expanding and developing the facilities. An extra yard was built in the village and the total capacity more than doubled. Ex-Champion Jockey, Sir Gordon Richards was persuaded to move from what is now Peter Makin's yard at Ogbourne Maisey to become the first tenant of the newly refurbished Whitsbury.

Gordon Richards remained at Whitsbury for five seasons and was, by all accounts, very happy there. He particularly revered its gallops, which, he maintained, were the best private gallops in the country (quite a compliment, given his experience of the magnificent facilities at Beckhampton). Despite training some good horses in the five years he worked at Whitsbury (including the game Reform, who won the St James's Palace, the Sussex, the Queen Elizabeth II, and the Champion Stakes in 1967) the relationship with his landlord deteriorated and, after failing to find anywhere as good as Whitsbury to train his large string, Sir Gordon gave up training in 1969.

Hill obviously decided that the leasing of the yard did not allow him sufficient control, so in 1970, the year before William Hill's death, Bill Marshall was installed as private trainer (although he was allowed to train for other owners, he remained a salaried employee). During the five years he spent at Whitsbury, Bill Marshall increased his string from 56 to 110, enjoying some notable successes with horses like Polacca and Grey Mirage.

Despite its age, it is really only in the last ten years that Whitsbury has become a household word, due to the dual purpose talents of its latest tenant, David Elsworth. When David Elsworth moved to Whitsbury from Colerne, it was one of the few leaseable yards able to accommodate his rapidly expanding string.

During the course of the decade, David Elsworth has been one of the few trainers who has achieved success consistently under both codes. Although to begin with, the jumpers were pre-eminent (Elsworth's Cheltenham team of 1983 was particularly memorable) the tables have gradually turned so that today the flat horses are in the ascendancy. When Elsworth's string arrived, it was the first time that National Hunt horses had been trained at Whitsbury for a number of years. The adaptation, however, was painless. Although a single gallop was sacrificed for a schooling ground, the remaining, famously stiff, Whitsbury gallops proved ideal stamina-building territory for the likes of Combs Ditch, Robin Wonder and a certain grey horse, who was among the first batch to be schooled over the new fences.

The blossoming of Desert Orchid's high profile career inevitably had an effect on the privacy of the yard. At the height of his fame, a gaggle of people could nearly always be found at the entrance to the lower yard, where the great crowd pleaser was stationed in full view of his adoring fans, a clever move from a trainer who has had to become the ringmaster of a media circus in addition to his role as a trainer of racehorses. Erstwhile Derby favourite, Seattle Rhyme - a star in his own right - now occupies the old boy's box, but it's not quite the same without him.

Mares in the Whitsbury Manor Stud paddocks.

Top class hurdler, Oh So Risky, surveys the scene in the bottom yard.

During the 1992 flat season, plans were cemented for a link-up between Whitsbury and nearby Whitcombe Manor Racing Stables. Peter Bolton has taken over David Elsworth's business and the joint operation now has access to both yards. The combination of Whitsbury's famous gallops and the state of the art facilities at Whitcombe Manor should make the joint operation, in whatever form it takes, a force to be reckoned with.

PAST TRAINERS:
Norman Scobie; Monty Smyth; Sir Gordon Richards; Bill Marshall; James Bethell.

NOTABLE HORSES:
Reform; Desert Orchid; Floyd; Combs Ditch; Robin Wonder; In the Groove; Barnbrook Again; Oh So Risky; Indian Ridge; Seattle Rhyme.

OWNERS:
Sheikh Ahmed Al Maktoum; Ecurie Foustok; Raymond Tooth; Sir Hugh Dundas; Barry Hearn; Walter Maritti; Ray Richards; T. Lightbowne

Norton Grange, Malton.

Jimmy Fitzgerald

When racing people talk about Malton, they mean Norton. Anyone who has been to this great horse trading/training centre knows that 'things racing' only really begin once you have crossed the railway bridge into Malton's silent other half, Norton. Traditionally, the great training establishments associated with the town - Whitewall, Highfield House, Spring Cottage - have been sited on the south side of the town, close to the public training grounds at Langton Wold. In recent years, however, one of the largest and most successful stables to have come under the banner of Malton has been found in Norton itself, within sight of the railway tracks that divide the two communities.

Norton Grange is the creation of one Jimmy Fitzgerald, Yorkshire racing's most famous adopted son, who has turned what was essentially a rambling mixed farm into one of the best known racing stables in the north of England. After giving up riding, Jimmy Fitzgerald had no intention of taking up training: "It was always my specific intention not to go into training and I went two years without saddling a horse. I knew only too well what a hassle the business was, and I must say I've been proved absolutely right".

Jimmy Fitzgerald and the mare, Creselly.

At the beginning, in the late 1960s, Norton Grange had no facilities for the training of racehorses. The land now used as gallops was a cornfield and livestock occupied what was then a rambling farmyard but which has since become an extensive expanse of varied stabling, barns and loose boxes. Sixty bullocks lived in what is now the main barn.

"The place just grew with me" says the Master of Norton Grange, in his nonchalant way. "Being in Malton, one or two people started offering me horses and the second horse that we ran, Archer, won a novice hurdle at Market Rasen and then won again a week later at Southwell". In stages, the farmyard became a racing yard. Many of the boxes were built by the trainer himself: "I paid the bricklayer two shillings an hour and I laboured for him. I think the cost was about £25 per box".

At that time, Bill Elsey and his Highfield stable were the power in the land at Malton, followed by Pat Rohan, Bill Dutton and Frank Carr and flat racing was very much the dominant code. The nascent stable in a corner of a farmyard at Norton Grange did not even register on the scale. Gradually the situation changed. The two winners of 1969 were followed by eight the next year, twelve the year after that and twenty eight in 1972. Some established owners began to send a few interesting prospects to Norton Grange, and by the end of the decade, Jimmy Fitzgerald had become one of the leading jumping trainers in the north, a position he has consolidated ever since, developing also into a formidable trainer of flat horses.

Fitzgerald Junior and Senior at work..

As is so often the case in the intensely lived activity of National Hunt racing, where triumph is commingled with tragedy, there have been some amazing twists and turns of fate along the way. No story illustrates this more effectively than the remarkable story of Fairy King, a young chaser that Jimmy Fitzgerald believed was the best he had ever trained.

"He had so much ability that I was convinced that, given a bit of luck, he could have beaten anything in the country. We had taken him to Kempton to get an idea of whether we should run him in the King George or not and he broke his back in a fall at the second last. It was, without doubt, the worst day in my training career, the kind of day that makes you wonder what on earth are you doing in this game. After the fall, the agony was prolonged because they wouldn't let me have him put out of his misery straight away. I could see that his back was broken and he kept looking at me as if to say, why can't I get up? It was awful."

This darkest of dark clouds, however, had a silver lining, in the unlikely shape of Barney Curley. "Barney came over to see me on the day that the horse was killed. He said that he felt sorry for me and that he had a horse that would go some way towards filling the gap". The horse was Forgive 'n' Forget.

"I went over to see the horse and you knew from the first minute that you saw him that this was a potential champion. He was a lovely looking horse, beautifully sound. Having said that he was an absolute bugger to ride sometimes".

Like so many top class horses, Forgive 'n' Forget was an alert, inquisitive horse at home. According to his trainer, he liked to be able to see the activity of the yard: "We put him in the box by the road, so he could see what was going on inside the yard and outside". From Forgive 'n' Forget's old vantage point, the light industrial fringe of the town is plainly visible. It is a bustling place, where horses quickly get used to the noise they will inevitably encounter on

Fitzgerald talks tactics with jockey Mark Dwyer.

the racecourse. And yet, on the other side of the yard, the open fields extend as far as the eye can see, to Whitewall and the training grounds of Langton Wold beyond.

Jimmy Fitzgerald is a great believer in Malton as a place to train horses. "I honestly believe it's the best place in the country to train. The gallops are nicely on the collar so you don't have to work horses into the ground to get them fit. It's also a great centre geographically: there are nine racetracks within one hour's drive of Malton. I would give up training if I had to go to Newmarket".

After spending any length of time with Jimmy Fitzgerald, it soon becomes apparent why he has succeeded in forging a successful business where so many others have failed. In addition to his undoubted qualities as a horseman, he has a wry detachment from the pressures of the game and a determination to enjoy his chosen way of life that must help to see him through the difficult times. "Training is such an out and out pleasure when they're all healthy, watching them work and bringing young horses along", he enthuses in his inimitable brogue.

Any prospective owner could be sure that not only would their charge be well looked after and placed to advantage at Norton Grange but that ownership with J. Fitzgerald would be fun into the bargain.

PREVIOUS TRAINERS:
None

NOTABLE HORSES:
Forgive 'n' Forget; Canny Danny; Fairy King;
Galway Blaze; Kayzee; Fairy King;
Magic Tip; Sapience; Trainglot;
Uncle Ernie; Sybillin.

OWNERS:
A.F. Budge (Equine) Limited; Lord Halifax; Marquesa De Moratella;
Mr.R. Haggas; Norman Jackson; J. Dick; W.A. Farrell;
Robinson Publications Ltd; Kenton Utilities;
Halewood Vintners; C.H. Hartley; Mrs A. Leggatt;
Mrs K.D. Leckenby; Mrs.M. Curtis; Paul Coulter;
Mrs D.B. McGowan; John A. Cooper; J. McCaghy;
A.Ryan; Mrs H. Ogden; Barry Winfield;
D. Bowker; C.Marner; Mrs B. Eve; Mrs Margaret.
M. Brock; J.S. Murdoch; Peter Hall; Joseph Ogden;
A.J.Hogan; Ronald Howe; P.Asquith; A. Soulsby; Mrs.F. Patten;
T.J. Acott; Kilroe Group; Bezwell Fixings; A.D .Bottomley;
J.W.P. Curtis; A. Bayman; Mrs Dorothea Dickson;
Phoenix Waterproofing; R.L. White

Old Manor House, Letcombe Bassett.

Captain Tim Forster

FIFTY SIX WINTER seasons have passed since Golden Miller set out from his new home at the Old Manor House yard at Letcombe Bassett one cold March morning to make the customary four mile trudge to Wantage Station. The destination that day was Cheltenham, where Dorothy Paget's legendary chaser recorded his fifth and last Gold Cup victory, the Welsh partnership of trainer, Owen Anthony and jockey, Evan Williams taking over from Basil Briscoe and Gerry Wilson.

Half a century later, only a dwindling few remember the celebrations that followed in the Yew Tree, the local pub, but such is the continuity of this close-knit racing village that the grandson of the man who put the plates on Golden Miller that day, Len Abrahams, still shoes horses in the yard today. It is that kind of place.

For the last thirty years, the trainer at the Old Manor House yard has been one of the stalwarts of the winter game, namely "The Captain", Tim Forster, who himself has become part of Letcombe Bassett folk-lore. A painting on the office wall, donated in gratitude by the villagers of Letcombe Bassett themselves, testifies to the not inconsiderable feat of bringing "three Grand National winners to the village". "A big winner for the yard is a matter of shared pride for the village", according to the Captain.

This is no empty sentiment; in a village the size of Letcombe Bassett, where the local pub has been forced to close through lack of business, a thriving sixty box yard provides not only a major source of employment but a much needed focal point. Captain Forster is very much aware of the importance of the yard to the village and vice versa and, in addition to his duties as trainer, has been Chairman of the Parish Council for many years.

Physically, too, the yard is very much part of the village, the timber framing and thatched roof of the trainer's house and a cluster of eighteenth century farm buildings forming its core. The Parish Church of St Michael's and the churchyard where Golden Miller's trainer, Owen Anthony, lies buried, overlook the yard, surveying a scene essentially unchanged in two hundred years. In the distance, the yard's raison d'etre, the Downs, form a splendid natural amphitheatre.

The Captain and Well To Do's commemorative clump of trees.

The landscape of the Downs has changed considerably since the days of Owen Anthony and Golden Miller. Memories of working horses on Green Down and the surrounding area extend back even further, to the 1920's, when Letcombe Bassett was a remote village, particularly bleak and isolated in midwinter. The old Letcombe Bassett trainer, Tom Morgan, who trained for many years from Captain Forster's overspill yard at Ivy Lodge, first visited the village as a fourteen year old apprentice in 1920, and has vivid memories of one of Owen Anthony's predecessors.

"The trainer at the Old Manor House then was a Mr Robson. I'd come down to ride work on a horse he wanted me to ride at Gosforth Park later that week and he picked me up in a pony and trap from Wantage Station. He was more of a gentleman farmer than a trainer; he had hundreds and thousands of sheep on the surrounding hills. The Downs were very bare then, not cultivated like they are today, which meant that the old turf was perfect for working horses on". In those halcyon days before the advent of mass tourism and the tractor, even the path of the Ridgeway itself was used as a gallop.

Since Captain Forster's arrival in the early 1960's, changes in agriculture have meant the virtual disappearance of sheep from the Downs and the gradual encroachment of arable farming. Hard-up trainers, too, did not take too much persuading, in an era of seemingly ever increasing subsidies, to sell off their gallops to the Barley Barons. Standing on the Ridegway above Letcombe Bassett, those with long memories could point out a disturbing number of formerly magnificent gallops that have been lost, perhaps forever, to the plough.

Even those that survive do not have a guaranteed future. Even a traditionalist such as Captain Forster, who has spent most of his working life on the Downs, views the tending of private gallops as "the most appallingly expensive form of amusement". Only half in jest, he continues,

The Old Manor House (right) in the last century.
The entrance to the yard is on the right.

The traditional face of a modern yard: the office fits neatly at one end of an old weatherboarded barn.

"I could probably dispense with them and spend the rest of my life watching horses trail four furlongs up an all weather strip. The only maintenance would be to drag a tractor up it at lunchtime". At present, the 80 acres of gallops attached to the Old Manor House yard, require the constant attention of a gallops man, mowing and tending in glorious isolation. "It's a pretty lonely job these days. In the past, he could pass the time of day with any number of people working on the land. Nowadays, he'd be lucky to see anybody all day once we've gone home".

Head lad, David Cooper and novice chaser, Hearts are Wild.

Thankfully, the Captain is unlikely to dispense with his superb inheritance of working ground. "I think I would go mad working in the same place every day. You have to think about the quality of working life apart from anything else". The success of trainers relying solely on all weather gallops has not convinced the Captain that the days of grass gallops are over. "Mr Pipe has shown that it can be done but who's to say that he wouldn't have done even better with a greater variety of gallops. Even a forward thinker like Michael Dickinson thought that some of the mossy turf that we have here could not be bettered anywhere in England".

Neither has Captain Forster entirely forsworn other of the time-honoured but increasingly endangered rituals associated with the training of steeplechasers. "I'm probably too long in the tooth to change but I still believe in the virtue of long canters and trotting. One of the reasons why people came to this area to train in the first place, apart from the ground, was the variety of surrounding hills. Sincombe Hill in particular is a wonderful trot; a steady pull-up for a mile and a half every day up there for six weeks in September and October is, in my view, an ideal preparation for the season".

That the trainer of Well To Do, Ben Nevis and Last Suspect should feel obliged to defend the pre-season trotting of horses is a sure sign of changing times. The method has certainly worked effectively enough for the past thirty years. There are few National Hunt trainers on the increasingly competitive southern circuit who have managed to sustain such a consistently solid level of achievement. Seemingly heedless of fashion, Captain Forster has gone on producing old fashioned staying chasers of the highest calibre, the reward being the continuing loyalty of the kind of patrons that most trainers would give their eye teeth for. The sight of one of Captain Forster's chasers staying on through the mud - preferably bearing the lovingly handwashed Arkle colours of Anne, Duchess of Westminster - is one of the more enduring sights of the National Hunt scene. Long may he continue.

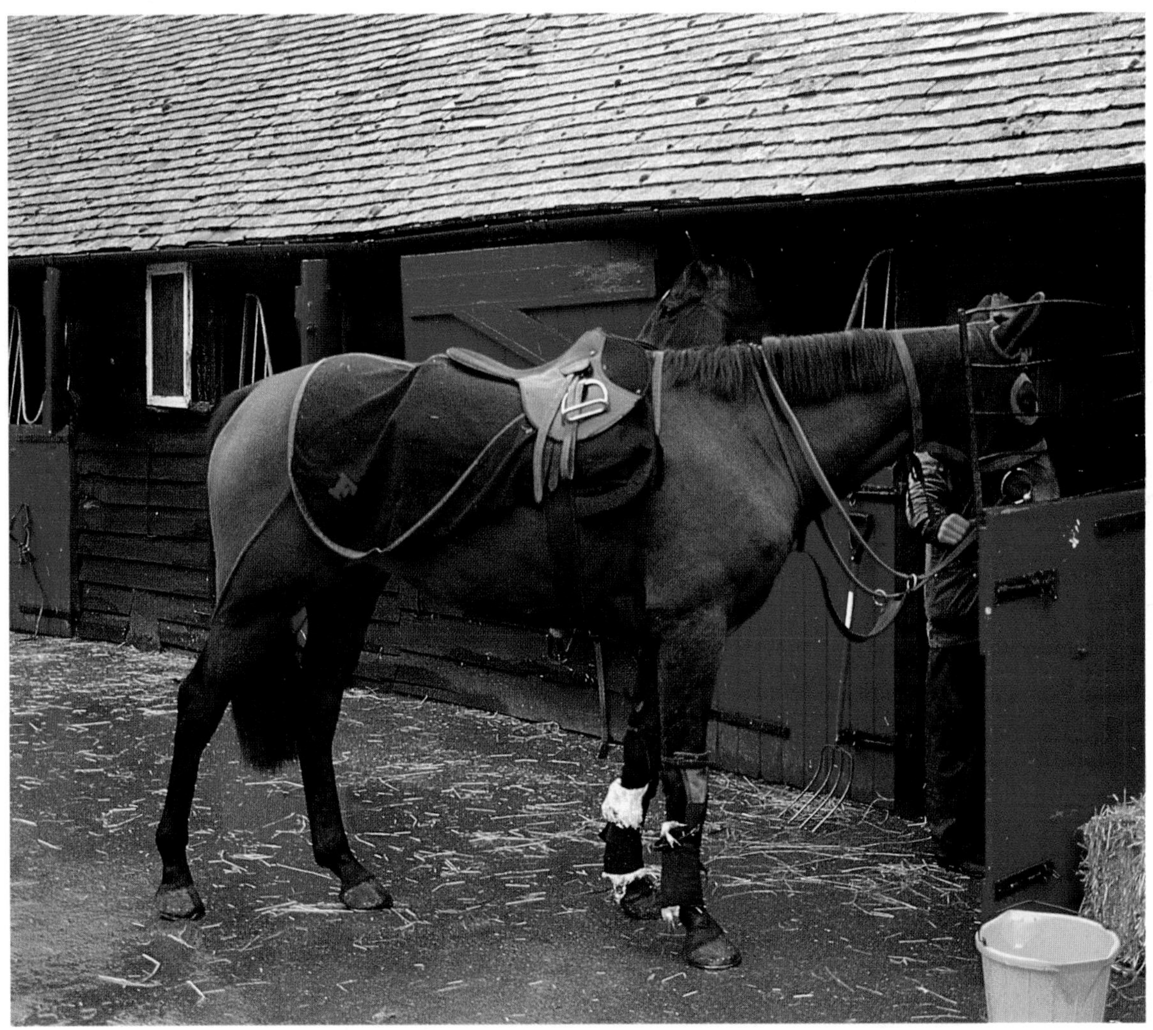

A characteristic Letcombe Bassett scene: a young chaser returns from an early season workout.

Glen Cherry keeps an eye on the neighbours.

PAST TRAINERS:

G. Spittle; Edward Robson; Major Miller; Owen Anthony; Buck Hammond; Arthur Garner; T.H. Yates

OWNERS:

Anne Duchess of Westminster; Simon Sainsbury; Lady Pilkington; Gregory Phillips; John Sumner; Lord Chelsea; Lord Cadogan; Lord Leverhulme; Col.Sir Piers Bengough; Countess of Eglinton & Winton; C.V.MacSwiney; Lady Knutsford; The Royal Hussars; Miss.J. Abel Smith; Brigadier C.B. Harvey; Lt.Col.R.B. Merton; Exors of the late Mrs J.de.Rothschild; Mrs A. Reid Scott; Mrs P.B. Mitford-Slade; Major A.K. Barlow; T.F.F.Nixon; Nigel Harris; H.K. Padfield; Mrs D.K. Price; Mrs A.S. Clowes; Mrs Jeremy Cotton; Mrs M. Ward-Thomas; J.R.Adam; Mrs G.C.McFerran; Mrs G.W. Lugg; G.W. Cleaver; Lady Zetland; Sir Philip Payne-Gallwey.

PAST ASSISTANTS:

Tim Thomson Jones; Kim Bailey; Mark Smyly; Graham Thorner

NOTABLE HORSES:

Preface; Residue; Golden Miller; Roman Hackle; Solford; Limb of the Law; Well To Do; Ben Nevis; Last Suspect; Pegwell Bay.

HORSE TO FOLLOW:

Plat Reay

Downs House, Findon.

Josh Gifford

AS LONG AGO as 1896, *Racing Illustrated* magazine described Downs House Stables, Findon - "on the chalk hills on the road from Worthing to Horsham" - as "well built, airy and exceedingly comfortable, good enough, indeed, for the presence of horses of the very highest class". The accompanying photograph shows a neat, flint-walled stableyard, the smartly dressed lads blinking in the low sun of a winter's morning, with an ivy clad Downs House just visible beyond.

Remarkably little has changed in the hundred years or so since those words were written; although the amount of stabling at Downs House has increased considerably, the main yard is as serviceable as ever and remains virtually unaltered. In 1896, the yard's history as a racing stable had hardly begun. The then trainer, a Mr F. Barratt, described in *Racing Illustrated* as "a man who thoroughly understands his business", trained chiefly on the flat, achieving some success in handicaps such as the Great Metropolitan at Epsom, which were much more prestigious at the time than now.

Josh Gifford and stable jockey, Declan Murphy.

Downs House, Findon did not really carve a recognisable niche for itself in the history of the turf until the early years of this century, when the National Hunt trainer, Bobby Gore, set out his stall as a notable handler of staying chasers. One horse in particular stands out, the gallant Jerry M, who finished a close third in the Grand National of 1910 as a seven year old under the welter burden of 12-7 and then went on to win it, two years later, under the same weight. Gore's prowess as a trainer was confirmed the next year, when Jerry M's stable companion, Covertcoat, won the National by a distance. Both were owned by one of the yard's main patrons, Sir Charles Assheton-Smith, and sired by one of the most influential stallions of the period, Hackler.

Gore trained at Findon for the next two decades, although by the mid 1930s his string numbered barely a dozen horses, mostly owned by his patron, Lord Abergavenny. The war brought a complete halt to the stable's activities, with a consignment of Canadians billeted in the house. It was not until the arrival in the early 1950s of perhaps Findon's most famous son, Captain H.R. Price, that stable fortunes began to turn.

Within three years of arriving at an empty yard, Price was training a larger string - 45 horses - than had ever been trained at the yard before. His successor at Downs House, Josh Gifford, who first arrived at the yard somewhat later, as an apprentice in 1958, remembers his former boss as "a hard man. His bark was worse than his bite but nevertheless, we were all terrified of him, but if he liked you, you'd be all right. You could never be sure of him though because as soon as he thought you were getting too confident, he'd knock you right down again".

The Captain was a prolific source of winners in every class of National Hunt race. According to his stable jockey, the great Fred Winter, quoted in the latter's biography, "he enjoyed winning a race at Devon and Exeter just as much as winning a big one at Cheltenham". This is borne out by the unprecedented number of jumping winners sent out by the yard; Price was the Martin Pipe of his day, sending out a record 71 winners in the mild winter of 1952-53. The somewhat unlikely combination of the loud, irrepressible Ryan Price and his more taciturn stable jockey, Fred Winter, proved irresistible. Together they won three Champion Hurdles and a Grand National.

Schooling on the Findon downs.

The winners did not stop when Fred Winter retired to take up training. His successor as stable jockey, Josh Gifford, quickly struck up an equally succesful partnership with the Captain, breaking Winter's record of jumping winners in a season. After getting too heavy to ride on the flat allowing a fruitful apprenticeship with Sam Armstrong at the St Gatien yard in Newmarket, Gifford took every opportunity that came his way at Downs House. "When I made the move, I came all the way from Newmarket in the horsebox to the races, where I met the boss. I'd just got my licence and he said to me 'ride that thing of mine in the maiden'. It was Eborneezer. Afterwards, I met John Sutcliffe and Paul Kelleway and we all went out on the razzle and I thought, 'this place is all right!'."

It was not all plain sailing. In 1964, the Captain was warned off indefinitely for the running of a horse called Rosyth, which had won the Schweppes Gold Trophy at Liverpool two years in succession, but had been unplaced, suspiciously in the view of the stewards, on four occasions in between. For everyone at Downs House, the sentence came as a complete shock.

Diminutive Victorian stable lads at work in the flint-walled yard.

"It didn't sink in at first" according to Gifford. "but then we found that there were cameramen hiding in hedges by the gallops the next morning. It was a terrible time. We continued to ride out every morning as though nothing had happened but gradually the horses started to disappear until we were left with about half a dozen from 80". The general feeling in the industry was that the sentence had been overly severe and, to the satisfaction of everyone in the jumping community, Price's licence was restored the following season.

By the end of the decade, Price had begun to switch his attention to the flat, gradually increasing the quantity and quality of the two year old intake every year. One day, Gifford remembers "we were walking up the hill and the guv'nor said to me 'what are you going to do when you pack up?' I was taken aback because I thought he was implying that I had lost my nerve or something. Anyway, I mumbled something about training and he said 'what about this place?' I didn't know what to say and he said 'I'll give you half an hour to think about it'. He wanted £29,000, which I didn't have and he said that I could pay him £9,000 with the rest at five grand a year interest free".

A busy day's schedule chalked on the board in the tack room.

From that moment on, Gifford trained the jumpers at Downs House, while Price moved down the hill to Soldiers' Field, where he specialised in the flat. "We had terrible battles about the gallops" remembers Gifford, who, unlike his mentor, never developed an interest in the other code. At the outset of his long and distinguished training career, Josh Gifford had just 30 horses, "the boss nicked all the good ones", a figure that has now risen to a fairly constant 70 (the capacity at Downs House itself is 60). Originally, the property consisted of just half a house, six acres and the yard but since the death of Captain Price, the Downs House estate has

Saddling up in an unchanged main yard today.

been expanded to include all the gallops and schooling grounds, which must be the equal of those available to any National Hunt trainer in the country. In addition, thanks to the characteristic generosity of his late longstanding patron, Mr Joel, Josh Gifford now has the use of the whole of Downs House, eloquent testimony to their happy and fruitful association over the years.

PAST TRAINERS:
F. Barratt; R. Gore; Bobby Bates;
Captain Ryan Price

PAST ASSISTANTS:
John Sutcliffe; Guy Harwood; Merrick Francis;
James Fanshawe; Paul Nicholls

NOTABLE HORSES:
Jerry M; Covertcoat; Royal Falcon; Clair Soleil; Fare Time; Eborneezer; Kilmore;
Beaver II; What A Myth; Kybo; Paddyboro; Aldaniti; Bradbury Star; Deep Sensation

OWNERS:
Maurice Pinto; Mr and Mrs S.N.J. Embiricos, Pell-mell Partners;
Capt.Tyrwhitt-Drake; Timothy Pilkington; Mrs Heather Alwen; S.D. Musson;
Miss.J. Semple; Mrs.F. Welch; R.F. Eliot; James Campbell; Mrs S.A.Willis;
G.T. Radmore; Mrs.T.F. Bliss; P.G. James; H.T. Pelham; Raymond Anderson
Green; Ken Carr; Bill Naylor; I. Kerman; Mrs Russell Bowes; Frank Arthur;
Mrs.P. Jubert; A. Ilsley; Leonard Simpson; Barry Fearn; P. Langmead;
Mrs.I. Spellar; P.G. Simcock; Mrs E.N. Tufnell; W.E.Gale;
Miss N. Hughes; Mrs.C. Clatworthy.

HORSES TO FOLLOW:
Martin's Lamp; Rainbow Castle

Seven Barrows, Lambourn.

Nicky Henderson

June 1992 saw the end of an era at Seven Barrows, as Peter Walwyn's string turned right out of the gate for the last time to make the long walk down the road to Windsor House, Lambourn, where the former champion trainer's career had begun more than twenty years before.

It must have been a poignant moment, but for Nicky Henderson, whose sizeable string had long been bursting at the seams at Windsor House, the opportunity to swap yards with the Walwyns was heaven sent. "It would have been impossible to sell Windsor House in the present climate and the chance to move somewhere like Seven Barrows doesn't come up every day. I'd been looking to move for some time. When Barry Hills was trying to put together a Manton rescue package, I'd gone a long way down that road but the move to Seven Barrows was absolutely ideal, in that it involved very little disruption for the staff".

Nicky Henderson and Muffin on the lawn at their spacious new home.

Seven Barrows, which derives its name from a collection of Saxon burial mounds on the site, has long been one of Berkshire's leading yards: "the ideal of a secluded training establishment", according to a nineteenth century account. It is a singular place, once removed from Lambourn and the gossipy conviviality of the shared public gallops.

The main house at Seven Barrows in the nineteenth century.

The Henderson string make their way home past the eponymous barrows (above), the landscape noticeably less barren than in the 1940s. (below)

The first noteworthy horse to be trained at Seven Barrows was Bendigo, who was purchased by his owner, Captain 'Buck' Barclay, as a mount for a 'Hunters' flat race. Trained by a Pickwickian character called Charles Jousiffe, a larger than life man, who was forever boasting about the chances of his horses, Bendigo turned out to be one of the sturdiest and most consistent horses of his generation. He was a late developing horse and after winning the Cambridgeshire at three, he went on to win the Champion Stakes (two days after coming second in the Cesarewitch), and the first ever Eclipse at Sandown among many other victories.

The next good horse that Jousiffe trained proved to be the death of him. Surefoot, an unusually large and muscular colt, won the 2,000 Guineas of 1890 very easily and was made an odds-on favourite for the Derby. Sadly, Surefoot's temperament got the better of him and the horse never won another race for Jousiffe, who died later that year (the lych gate of the parish church in Lambourn was erected in his memory). After Jousiffe's death, the yard was taken over by Garrett Moore, who George Lambton remembered fondly as the "steeplechasing lot's champion against all these flat racing swells". Moore's most significant achievement in racing was to coax one more good performance from Surefoot, who won the next year's Eclipse for his new trainer.

Sparkling Flame leads Remittance Man.

After a quiet period in the Edwardian era, Seven Barrows rose to prominence in the racing world once again after the First World War, when a self-made Lancastrian financier called James White bought the estate and installed the Cheshire trainer, Harry Cottrill as his private trainer. Cottrill outstayed his hard gambling patron, who killed himself after the stock market crash in the 1920s, and set about developing the yard into one of the top training establishments in the country. Cottrill's class of patron improved immeasurably and in its heyday in the late thirties, Seven Barrows numbered most of the leading nobility among its owners, including such notable racing figures as the Earl of Derby, Lady de Trafford and Vicomte Foy. In its heyday, Seven Barrows was much larger even than its present day incarnation. Harry Cottrill had access to both sides of the famous Farringdon Road (the left hand side now forms part of Barry Hills' South Bank estate) in addition to Moss Hill (now Matty McCormack's main gallops) and other work grounds that have now reverted to farmland.

Both Seven Barrows and the neighbouring racing yard at Kingstone Warren were leased from the Craven estate until 1958, when the Craven family got into financial difficulties and had to sell off much of their land. Both Seven Barrows and Kingstone Warren were purchased by the Craven family's former tenant, Major Derrick Candy (father of Henry Candy), who changed the boundaries between the two, enlarging Kingstone Warren at the expense of Seven Barrows. Until that point, Kingstone Warren had always played second fiddle to Seven Barrows, but now positions were reversed.

It was not until Peter Walwyn arrived in the mid 1960s, and started to achieve some notable successes on the racetrack, that Seven Barrows began to claw back some of its old prestige. Under Walwyn, the estate was restored to something like its former glory. Success meant more horses and this in turn resulted in extra accommodation for the lads, extended stabling and greatly improved facilities, including a covered ride and an indoor school.

Circling on the downs in the late Victorian era.

Looking across the attractive main yard, which dates from Peter Walwyn's era.

For Walwyn's successor, Nicky Henderson, the move to Seven Barrows has been "like being reborn. We're totally in our own domain here, everything is under one roof, so to speak, and the gallops are, quite simply, different class. The quality of the turf is just excellent". The principal working ground at Seven Barrows is the famous Farringdon Road gallop, a magnificent mile and a half straight which, according to its enthusiastic new owner, "never stops climbing. It's a relentless piece of ground, beautifully on the collar the whole way". In addition, there is the cantering ground at Pit Down and "masses of other ground", some of which has been made into a schooling ground, the first fences seen at Seven Barrows for many a year.

The management of such a large expanse of private ground represents a significant development in Nicky Henderson's training career. At Windsor House, the only private land apart from the yard was a single ten acre paddock. "It's certainly going to be a challenge. At the moment, I'm desperately trying to recall my year at Cirencester, digging out all my notes on grass management and potato picking!". If Peter Walwyn's experience is anything to go by, mole catching is another discipline to be boned up on.

Pre-Walwyn days.

The new Master of Seven Barrows does not anticipate any radical change in training methods. "Obviously, we've got to learn how to use the gallops but I remember some

Looking back home through the trees from below the Farringdon Road gallop, newly graced with the heavy tread of the three mile chaser.

good advice that Fred Winter once gave me. It was after I'd been training on my own for four or five years and nothing was going right and I asked him where I was going wrong. He just said, 'whatever you do, don't start doing anything different, just for the sake of it'. He was quite right, there's no right or wrong way to train. Look at the two most successful National Hunt trainers in recent years: Martin Pipe and Michael Dickinson. Total opposites but both great successes".

PAST TRAINERS:
C. Jousiffe; Garrett Moore; H. Cottrill; W.H. Payne; David Hastings; Peter Walwyn

NOTABLE HORSES:
Bendigo; Surefoot; Adam's Apple; Lovely Rosa; Zucchero; Humble Duty; Grundy; Polygamy

OWNERS:
Baroness Hamer of Alford; Mrs Robert Sangster; Lord Pembroke; W. Shand-Kydd; Michael Buckley; Robert Waley-Cohen; Raymond Tooth; Chris Brasher; Hon.Mrs.Ian Wills; Lord Matthews; Roger Chapman; Lord Mostyn;Mrs Christopher Wells; Mrs J.A. Debenham; James H. Stone; Sheikh Amin Dahlawi; W.H.Whitbread; Lady Bevan; Irving Struel; Christopher Heath; D. Sieff; Mrs Hugh Maitland Jones; Saeed Manana; Lord Grimston of Westbury; R.V. Shaw; Mrs E. Roberts; Edward Winfield; R.J. Parish; W.A. Fagan; Erik Thorbek; M.Arbib; A.J.H. Reed; A.M. Ennever; Mrs E. Roberts; Peter Oldfield; J.E.H. Collins; Chandler Hargreaves; Stewart Wilson; J.R. Henderson

Sandhill, Somerset.

Philip Hobbs

Philip Hobbs' Somerset yard is imbued with the traditional flavour of National Hunt racing. Like his West Country hero, John Thorne (for whom he rode that grand chaser Artifice) Philip Hobbs is one of that old fashioned paradoxical breed that used to characterise National Hunt racing: a thoroughgoing professional horseman, for whom horses are a whole way of life, but who nevertheless revels in the Corinthian spirit of what is after all only a sport.

Unlike many ex-jump jockeys who simply drift into training because they can't think of anything else, Philip Hobbs had ambitions to train "ever since I turned pro at the age of 21". "Initially I wanted to try my hand in Lambourn, but the cost of renting a yard there as opposed to the rent on the family farm at Sandhill was prohibitive, so I came back home but I still had to spend all the money I had converting this place". With a degree of foresight untypical of the 'manãna' ethos prevalent among many jump jockeys, much of the advance preparation for Hobbs' training career took place well before his retirement. "At the end of my riding career, I rode work for a number of Lambourn trainers not so much to get rides but just to see how they went about things and the gallops here were put down three years before I gave up".

Horseshoes not arithmetic at the Sandhill Academy.

Sandhill, which lies in glorious countryside in the shadow of the Quantocks, a stone's throw from the North Somerset coast, is an ancient Crown Farm with no history of professional training, but for many years, Philip's father, Tony, held a permit to train and sent out a number of good horses in the family colours. So, although there were no facilities at Sandhill for coping with a large string, at the time he took out a licence to train, Philip, who has lived at Sandhill since he was seven years old, was familiar with all the techniques used by his father in the locality for getting horses fit: the forestry walks, the beaches and a steep field of old turf reclaimed from the Moor, where horses could be exercised safely in extreme weather conditions.

The process of transforming Sandhill from a farm with a few horses into a racing yard with farming as a sideline has been gradual. As is so often the case with the fraught business of training, the actual beginning was something of a let down: "I was promised a lot but got bugger all". There were so few horses, that obtaining a licence from the Jockey Club required a bit of uncharacteristic subterfuge. "We had to bump up the numbers a bit. We had nine boxes but only six occupants".

Philip Hobbs installed the all weather strip at Sandhill at a cost of £30,000.

Housing the new inmates (there are now sixty horses in the yard) has hardly disrupted the appearance of the farm at all. Attractive, traditional farm buildings, such as the old cart horse stalls, barely needed any conversion at all and some old barns - unsuitable anyway for modern farming - were easily adapted to become American style horse barns. When numbers reached 25 in 1988, Philip decided that the existing gallops were insufficient and set about installing an all weather strip at a cost of around £30,000.

From small acorns: Sarah Hobbs congratulates husband Philip on the occasion of their first winner (and runner), North Yard.

Despite being in many ways a traditionalist in his approach to training, - Philip again cites John Thorne as a role model who "always got his horses looking fit and well through a lot of hard work" - the deceptively boyish Sandhill trainer remains engagingly open to new ideas. How many trainers would travel all the way from Somerset to Cockerham in Lancashire for an open day at another yard? "I think Jack Berry was a bit surprised that we'd come all that way, but he's very successful doing what he's doing and I think it's important to keep an open mind and see

Head lad, Mark Palmer, in front of Sandhill, a manor house dating from the Elizabethan period.

what other people are doing".

Although Hobbs has no intention of turning his attention to the training of sharp two year old flat horses, unlike many National Hunt trainers, he is not averse to buying horses 'off the flat' and sending them hurdling. "I buy all sorts: from untried horses and ex-flat horses to older chasers - sometimes the change of scenery can do them good. As long as a horse can win, I'll train it. I get a good deal of pleasure and satisfaction winning a novice hurdle at Newton Abbot with a bad legged horse. Training is all about assessing a horse's potential and finding the right class of race for it".

The old farm has expanded beyond recognition in recent years.

Philip Hobbs' current record places him in the top ten in the National Hunt trainers' league table in terms of number of races won, a record that is all the more remarkable when you consider that very few of Sandhill's runners cost more than £8,000 and many a good deal less. For most of Sandhill's owners,

Sarah Hobbs and Aswamedh record the yard's first flat winner.

however, who tend to be one or two horse people, that is nevertheless a considerable investment. The need to offer value for money, therefore, is a constant imperative but, more than that, for the kind of small owner with whom the yard is associated, owning a racehorse has to mean more than being a mere entry in 'Horses in Training'. It is an intimate involvement with a friendly, family-run set-up, something that seems to come quite naturally to Philip, his wife Sarah and their staff.

Watching Sarah - herself an international three day eventer in her youth - coming back from a local Pony Club show, replete with ponies and daughters clutching rosettes, proves that living with horses is manifestly much more than a mere business.

PAST TRAINERS:
Tony Hobbs

NOTABLE HORSES:
Bonanza Boy; Joint Sovereignty; Moody Man; Runway Romance

OWNERS:
Dr.O. Zawawi; N.C. Savary; R.J. Tory; Mrs Megan Webb; D.R. Price; Peter Horsbrugh; Capt. E.J. Edwards-Heathcote; B. Cooper; Peter Luff; Mrs Delamain; John Shedden; James Burley; Michael Burley; Rod Hamilton; Mrs A.G. Lawe; R. Broomhall; Miss J.Cunningham; F. Beer; R.Wright; E.C. Everleigh; P.J.Gwyn; J.A.Northover; Geoff Meadows; Peter Luff; M.T.Lockyer; G.J. Giddy; Anthony Palmer; G.N. Noye; B.J.D. Lewis; I. Shaw; Mrs R.O. Stead; D.J.M. Newell; T.C. Frost; Miss H.L. Cope; Mr A. Stoddart

HORSE TO FOLLOW:
Cru Exceptionnel

Bell House, Presteigne.

Richard Lee

Bell House still looks like a pub, thirteen years after last orders. Perched halfway up a steep Herefordshire hill, cheek by jowl with the main road to Presteigne and Wales, it is the unlikeliest setting imaginable for the training of racehorses. Only the horsebox parked outside in place of the brewers' lorry gives any clue to the change of proprietor.

According to Bell House's racing landlord, Richard Lee, his extraordinary racing stable, which clings to the side of the hill like a Portugese vineyard, "just happened". "At the beginning I thought we might have half a dozen point to pointers but it grew and grew". With the help of an early owner, who also happened to own a building business, a muddy slope was gradually transformed into a neatly graduated sequence of narrow but perfectly flat-surfaced yards, linked by a steep concrete path. One thing that a horse in training with Richard Lee soon learns how to do is cope with gradients.

Another major part of the Bell House education is roadwork, a necessity as well as a virtue when your gallops are three quarters of an hour's walk away. In many parts of Britain, this might be dangerous or become something of a chore, but in this stunningly beautiful stretch of country, replete with forestry commission tracks and roads where the fastest vehicle one is likely to encounter is a tractor, it is idyllic and can prompt even a Herefordshire-born countryman like Richard Lee to wax lyrical. "There's miles and miles of quiet unspoilt road around here. You could go a different way, seven days a week and you'd never get bored".

Carol and Richard Lee's roots are in the point-to-point scene and this is classic hunting and point-to-point country, with the Brampton Bryan and Bredwardine meets both within spitting distance. The hunting is, if anything, too good: "if you send a pack of hounds into some of these woods, I guarantee they'll come out with a fox each". Although Richard and his wife Carol have little time for country pursuits other than racing these days (Richard sometimes drives the box himself on racing days) past connections come in handy: the schooling fences are built by the local point-to-point course builder.

The boss sorting out the entries.

The main gallops, at nearby Rodd, amid spectacular wooded scenery, are leased from a local farmer - "In this climate, it's probably his best crop" - and in Spring, the lambs have

Carol Lee and her beloved Delius.

to be rousted out of the way before work can progress. The gallops are laid out across two broad fields, one steeply sloped and the other relatively flat. The string begin on the latter, breezing across for approximately four furlongs, before passing through a gate to face a stiff stamina-building climb for the final two furlongs. Like the roadwork, it is testing, particularly in wet weather, but Richard Lee is a believer in a hard routine. A new all weather gallop is now completed and has already proved its worth in a wet winter.

Getting horses fit and particularly the painstaking rehabilitation of injured horses has been the Lee trademark since the family firm made the transition from point to pointing in 1986. The transformation of the formerly wayward Swardean and the successful reintroduction of the brittle-legged former Dickinson star, Delius, endeared Lee to many in the National Hunt fraternity, who have made something of a habit of sending him bad-legged horses. Establishing such a reputation is a double-edged sword to those saddled with it: "I suppose we've made our name bringing back injured horses, paying attention to detail, but if there's one thing I can't bear about National Hunt racing it's the injuries. We've got a fantastic vet in Liam Kearns but I'm running a racing stable, not a hospital and I'd much rather have a yard full of horses that could run all year round".

Although, in his frustration, Richard Lee professes a desire to become a dual purpose trainer, with more flat horses, his background in point to pointing and, before that in Lambourn as a farrier, mark him out as a National Hunt type through and through. He is firmly wedded to the principle of an annual pilgrimage to Ireland for good jumping stock: "I go to Eddie Harty, then Liam Gleason in the south and love every minute of it".

Despite the rural isolation of the yard and hard financial times, a healthy level of patronage has continued to provide the financial ammunition for such trips, with high profile owners, the Hitchins, maintaining their support. Loyalty, both from owners and to long serving horses, who are spoken about like old friends, is a feature of the yard. Market Leader, a sweet natured

Richard Lee surveys a mixed crop of novice chasers and sheep.

twelve year old, who occupies the box nearest the house, is a case in point. After half a dozen years of plodding valiantly around the local gaffs (Ludlow, Bangor, Hereford) with a fair degree of success, his equally long-serving owner, Mr Ernie Flello, will eventually retire him to serve as a hack for his wife, who has taken up riding at her home in Abberley, at the age of 50 plus.

Curiously, the relatively local Flellos are not typical of the owners that the Lees attract. "They're mostly from the south east and London - I think we're too down to earth to attract the spivvy scrap metal dealer types and we're not a gambling yard either, as I know only too well what can go wrong".

PAST TRAINERS:
None

NOTABLE HORSES:
Delius; Swardean; Classic Statement; Market Leader

OWNERS:
M. Johnson; D. Coltart; G. Sweeney; J. Jackson; M. M. Allen; D. Harris; Mrs J. Morris; D. Edwards; B. Holt; F. Ayres; Mrs Elizabeth Hitchins; Mrs Nicola Shields; Mr J. Bowen; T.M.J. Curry; Nigel Lilley; J. Piercy; J.O. Beavan; R.L.C. Hartley; W. George; Tony Raggett; M.J. Fairbrother; J.H. Watson; D&M. Watkins; Faversham Racing Club; Osborne House Ltd; Bob Brazier; Mrs C.E. Feather; J. Watkins; Marten Julian; Ernie Flello; D. Zeff; W. Roseff; M Broke; M. Bateman

HORSE TO FOLLOW:
Tina's Missile

Bankhouse, Cholmondeley.

Donald 'Ginger' McCain

THE OLD BOY must think he's died and gone to heaven. Red Rum's new quarters in the leafy, hunting country of the Cholmondeley estate in Cheshire are a world away from the beach at Southport. The view from Don McCain's back door is a bit different too: in place of 'Chinese takeaways and a railway line', there is a very un-Southportian vista of open parkland, broken only by the picturesque sight of geese wintering on a mere.

For Don McCain, coming to Cheshire meant returning to his racing roots, having started his career in racing at Sandy Brow, Tarporley as a stable lad. "I realised the other day, when I was forced to do a bit of mucking out, that I'd been shovelling shit for forty five years!" Despite being a native of Southport, McCain is equally enthusiastic about his adopted county of Cheshire: "A lot of people knock it, saying that it's flat and boring but around here, it's great country, a real centre for hunting - they go across the land like blazes around here - and, as a result it's a very horsey area. There used to be a lot of trainers around here and up at Tarporley and now it seems to be on the way back with Francis Lee, Ann Hewitt and Alan Bailey all doing well".

The old magician himself. Red Rum gazes out across the yard at his new home.

For many years, the Cholmondeley Estate was famous for its jumpers, who were trained from Cholmondeley Stables by George Owen, who had a considerable string in the '40s and 50s and won the Grand National with Russian Hero in 1949. For a time in the mid 50s, Stan Mellor was the stable jockey. "They used to gallop in the park, through the woods and on the mosses, which were a bit like the tan gallops at Chantilly" according to McCain.

In recent years, however, until the McCains arrived two years ago, the estate had been famous more for its dairy cows than its racehorses. Don 'Ginger' McCain and his wife, Beryl, known to their friends as Conk, had been looking around all over the country for a new yard. "We literally looked everywhere: from Newmarket to Lambourn but I decided that I was a bit too long in the tooth for a training centre. I'd been independent for too long". Eventually, the

Don McCain with one of the fences used for schooling his chasers.

A typical cold and misty spring morning on the gallops at Cholmondeley.

estate agents, Strutt and Parker approached McCain with the offer of a tenancy of one of the farms on the estate. "Dairy farming had got so intensive around here that there was a problem with pollution and the estate was looking to diversify. I had been interested in the place for a while and jumped at the chance".

At that time, Bankhouse did not look very much like a racing yard. "There was a vehicle shed, some bull pens and a tie up for cattle". With some demolition, a good deal of conversion and a bit of newbuild, McCain has transformed the old cattle yard into a 40 box stable, complete with horsewalkers and a menage. The next problem was working out where the gallops would be: "We've 200 acres of grass here, in addition to all the woods, so we were spoilt for choice in a way". One particularly inviting slope was chosen for the laying of that sine qua non of modern training, the all weather gallop. "It's four and a half furlongs, which is a good stiff five anywhere else". In addition, for longer work, the string can gallop "twice around the bottom of the hill, then up, adjacent to the all weather, which is about two miles and two furlongs".

Schooling young chasers.

Walking quietly down the testing all-weather gallop at Cholmondeley on a misty winter morning.

"To me, the aim of National Hunt racing should be to produce good staying chasers. We've got some very nice staying horses from good families, but they inevitably need time. A lot of people panic half way through their preparation - it's easy to doubt when they're not winning hurdle races - but it's a question of keeping faith until they come to themselves".

"I'm a good buyer of horses and a bad seller. The market for National Hunt horses became very false in recent years, it was blown out of all proportion. The money being paid for a National Hunt store is only now coming back into line. Even 12 months ago, people were paying 25 and 30,000, whereas now between 4 and 12,000 is more the norm".

PAST TRAINERS:
(On the estate at Cholmondeley: George Owen)

NOTABLE HORSES:
Russian Hero (on the estate); Red Rum; Hotplate

OWNERS:
B.Scowcroft; John Singleton; W. Hargreaves; C.J. Black; Mrs E. Sharp; Robin Billingsley; Martin Jump; W. Bellamy; F.S. Markland; Halewood Vintners; John J. Gray; J. Thompson; Mrs Betty Finch; Nolan Hardman; Alan Crowshaw.

HORSE TO FOLLOW:
Hey Cottage

Jackdaws' Castle, Temple Guiting.

David Nicholson

Many idle dreams are discussed over a pie and a pint in the local pub, but few outlive the hangover. Jackdaws' Castle, a brand new training centre, perched high in the Cotswolds, is an impressive exception.

Four years ago, as David 'The Duke' Nicholson and his long-time owner, Colin Smith, were mulling over future plans outside their local, The Plough, Smith suddenly pointed to the steep hillside opposite and asked "whether gallops would work up there". It was a leading question. Smith, a property consultant, owned the land, the tenant of which was a farmer who no longer wanted to farm. "I was concerned about my rent money!"

Nicholson was taken aback: "The thought had never crossed my mind until that point", but after thinking about it for a moment, the trainer replied "I think it would be fantastic". After that, there was no stopping them; land agents, Knight, Frank & Rutley were approached, a plan formulated and within twelve months, detailed planning permission had been granted.

Colin Smith and David Nicholson go back a long way. It is twelve years since Colin's wife, Claire, persuaded her husband (in another bar - this time the Champagne Bar at the Cheltenham Festival) to buy a horse. Through a mutual friend, Jenny Mould, the Smiths were

King of the castle: the Duke and owners look out over the virgin grass gallops.

Second lot emerge from their brand new quarters and head off on private roads to the adjacent gallops.

introduced to David Nicholson and a four year old store purchased. Its name was Charter Party. "I think that set the tone for our relationship", remembers Smith, "I think I expected every other horse we bought to win the Gold Cup!"

At the time of Smith's original brainwave, David Nicholson was still training from his old base at nearby Condicote, the sprawling converted farm that had become a fixture of the National Hunt scene. The original intention had simply been to use the new gallops as an adjunct to Condicote but eventually, for a number of reasons, a wholesale removal to the new site presented itself as the best of all possible worlds.

Jackdaws' Castle was formally opened by its regular royal work rider.

Despite the affection that the Duke, and indeed Colin Smith, felt for the scene of so many past triumphs, the prospect of starting afresh in a purpose-built estate with new facilities was "a mouthwatering prospect". The move was also financially desirable because, like so many others in a recession-hit industry, David Nicholson's business at Condicote had run into difficulties. Colin Smith offered Nicholson 'an out', the lifeline being a position as salaried trainer in a dramatically expanded version of the original 'gallops idea'.

Jackdaws' Castle was to be much more than a set of gallops; Smith's ambitious idea was to create a state-of-the-art training centre with "modern testing facilities and top class veterinary input" at the heart of the new gallops. This was easier said than done. The site may have been

Back home along private roads.

ideal for gallops, with its steep gradients and exhilarating air, but it was so exposed that, for the creation of an extensive stable yard and living accommodation, it could hardly have been less auspicious. If the planners had failed to kill off the project for dominating the horizon, the winds would have sorted out any survivors.

The eventual solution to the problem also provides an explanation as to how the yard came to acquire its romantic appellation. Jackdaws' Castle is the local name for a small quarry that was once situated just over the crest of the hill on which the gallops are situated. The peak, the second highest in the Cotswolds, towers over the surrounding land to the extent that, on a clear day, you can see half of south west England. The scollop-shaped indentation of the old quarry provided the perfect solution to the difficulties of the site, protecting both the neighbours' views and the stable's inmates alike.

The same land that had proved ideal in the past for the siting of a shallow quarry, necessarily required a good deal of stone picking before it could be rendered suitable for grass gallops. No less than 5,000 tons of stone were removed from the site, according to David Humbert, the Director of Peter Banks Plant Ltd (who were also responsible for the all weather gallops at Manton) who were contracted to create the gallops. "We de-stoned the whole estate but the gallops had to be prepared to a very high standard for obvious reasons. We acquired some stone removing machines from Norway, which prepare the soil as you would for an arable crop. The first six inches of topsoil are drawn up into the machine, which is drawn behind a tractor. The soil is sieved over a series of rotating webs and the stones thrown into a hopper". After this process had been repeated and a special racing turf seed mixture sown, over 1,000 tons of peat were used to consolidate the surface.

It has been a Herculean effort, but well worth it, according to Nicholson, who describes his new home as "a lovely place to train. We're completely removed from the roads and you couldn't wish for better gallops. They're all very much on the collar, which means you don't have to put too much work into them".

Standing with Nicholson and an enthusiastic group of owners during second lot, surveying the bright green turf of the, then as yet unused, grass gallops, Colin Smith's grand project seems a confident and enlightened idea. Even in the depths of an apparently ever deepening recession, there is a spirit of optimism about Jackdaws' Castle that is reflected not only in the number of owners that have made the switch from Condicote but in the number of new owners that have been attracted. Early results indicate that their optimism could be rewarded, but Colin Smith is far too pragmatic to get carried away: "I don't think for a minute that I'm going to recoup my investment or anything like that but if we can stick it out until the next wave of wealth comes flushing through the UK, we'll be in a prime position to take advantage".

Wonder Man takes a pick of grass in a field above the yard, which nestles in a sheltered hollow.

PROPRIETOR:
Colin Smith

TRAINER:
David Nicholson

NOTABLE HORSES:
Waterloo Boy; Carobee; Thetford Forest; Another Coral

OWNERS:
Mrs C. Smith; Mrs J. Mould; Capt.J. Macdonald-Buchanan; G.C. Mordaunt; Lord Vestey; Mrs S. Catherwood; Mrs.G. Maxwell-Jones; G. Roach; Mrs.S. Robins; Brig.C.B. Harvey; Major R.V.H. Yule; Mrs G.M. Brisbane; Hon.M.W. Vestey; M.R. Deeley; Marquess of Northampton; J. Brown; R.J. Rymer; Mrs.J.M. Snell; M.R. Deeney; Mrs.L. Lovell; Mrs.E. Roberts; Mrs.H. Taylor; C. Nicholl; J. Wright; J.S. Rigby; J. Hobbs; S.R.J. Garretty; D.J. Rindsland; Mrs M.P. Sutton; Mr & Mrs.R.J. Skan; Mrs.J.M. Battersby; B.J. Brooks; D. Jackson; Mrs J. Hall; Mrs.P. Vernon; Mr & Mrs Maryan-Green; P.G. Lowe; Mrs M.J. Rogers; Mrs S.B. Lockheart; P.G. Hepworth; J.F. Horn; L. Hellstenius; J.A.H. West; Mrs A.J. Davies; Mrs.M.Kerr-Dineen; D. Gibbon; Ford Farm Bloodstock.

HORSE TO FOLLOW:
Travelling Wrong

Cree Lodge, Ayr.

Linda Perratt

British racing owes a lot to Scotland, but, unfortunately for the latter, its contribution has traditionally consisted largely of exports, both equine and human. From the Dawson and Waugh training dynasties of the past to present day jockeys like Willie Carson and Richard Quinn, Scottish talent has mostly reached fruition in England.

Today, the indigenous Scottish racing scene is a sadly reduced shadow of its former self. Once, over a hundred horses were trained on the sands at Ayr alone; now, not many more than that are trained professionally in the entire country. This is reflected in the local racing, which is mostly exceedingly modest, the bare minimum Levy Board prizemoney snaffled up almost exclusively by 'incomers', be they North of England trainers or pot-hunting Newmarket yards. At the 1992 Ayr Western meeting, the highpoint of the Scottish racing season, only three Scottish yards were represented and, of those, only Linda Perratt's Cree Lodge yard managed a place.

Today, Cree Lodge is Scotland's largest yard with around 30 horses in at any one time throughout the year. It was built in 1908, a year after Ayr racecourse moved to its present location, on what was described in a contemporary account as "150 acres of good sand soil

Former Cree Lodge trainer, Charlie Williams puts a two year old through a stalls test.

within five minutes of Ayr Station". At the time, there was no racecourse stabling and the yard had to double as accommodation for any runners coming from a distance.

'Johnny' and Persian Charmer.

Life in the yard at the time is unusually well documented thanks to the entertaining memoirs of Cree Lodge's founder, John McGuigan, doyen of Scots trainers in the interwar years, who trained at the yard for over half a century. McGuigan's vivid account of his own training career offers a rare insight into a very different era. "When I commenced to train, those in the profession had only recently been raised to a little higher status than that of 'training grooms' by which name they were known when they wore the livery of their employer at race meetings".

Although some of the training customs from the McGuigan era seem remote, others are surprisingly familiar, particularly those relating to horses' health. At the turn of the century, McGuigan's yard was struck down by a mystery virus: "The epidemic got all sorts of names, such as 'Newmarket fever' and 'Pink Eye' but it was nothing less than pneumonia - strong inflammation of the lungs - and when some of the animals were opened, we saw that their lungs were like a piece of tree bark". McGuigan's efforts to contain the outbreak were typically forlorn: "I had bags saturated with Jeyes fluid hanging at every box door and all sorts of disinfectant in every box to try and stop the spread of the disease"

Such outbreaks aside, Ayr was a flourishing training centre at the turn of the century, based around the use of the town's long stretch of golden sand as a training ground. McGuigan recalls a time "when there were over 100 doing work at Ayr". The old Cree Lodge trainer was certain of the virtues of working horses on the sand: "There is not the slightest doubt that sea air tones horses up, that shy feeders clean up their mangers after having been a little while by the sea, that salt water is excellent both for good and bad legged animals". By the end of McGuigan's career, just before the outbreak of war, the number of horses in training at Ayr had dwindled, and training eventually ceased altogether when hostilities commenced. "In 1943, there were no horses in training on Ayr Sands and somehow neither they nor the sporting old town seem the same without any blood 'uns in their clothing processing to the sea-shore".

Since the war, training has continued at Ayr without interruption, although the days of 100 horses exercising on the beach are long gone. Cree Lodge today is much the same as it was in McGuigan's day, although the advent of stabling at the racecourse over the road means that space no longer has to be found for visiting horses, as in the days when the old trainer's house was used "like a kind of turf club" for visiting owners and trainers.

The current trainer at the venerable old Cree Lodge Stables is Linda Perratt, the sixth trainer since the war, who, for three years prior to taking over the reins, was assistant to her predecessor, John Wilson. Wilson's company was liquidated in 1991, since when Linda Perratt and her father have formed their own company to run the yard, a brave move in such recessionary times. Their audacity has been rewarded with a healthy complement of 34 horses, which is not far off the yard's capacity. Robert McKellar, who was formerly travelling head lad to John Wilson, acts as assistant and former Cree Lodge trainer Charlie Williams, who still lives nearby, is an invaluable source of advice. Williams is a veteran Cree Lodge man, having been with Harry Whiteman as head lad and assistant for sixteen years before training in his own right at the yard for another seven.

Such continuity is typical of the close-knit Cree Lodge set-up. Training at Ayr has probably changed little since McGuigan's day. The majority of the everyday work takes place just over the road at the racecourse. There is a sand all weather track, measuring approximately a mile that runs right around inside the racetrack itself, as well as a broad strip of grass that is slightly more extensive. Apart from in the build up to the Western meeting, when a number of more southerly-based horses use the facilities if they are stationed overnight, Ayr racecourse provides virtually a private training ground for the Perratt string.

In addition to the main work grounds, Linda Perratt keeps up tradition by working her horses on the beach, "although they have to be off by nine o' clock to avoid knocking over the holidaymakers". The nearby Carrick Hills are another option for a change of scene. "We box them up and it's only a few minutes away, It helps to keep them interested". Linda is very much a hands-on trainer, a talented amateur rider in her own right, who clearly has an

First thing on the day of the Western meeting, and a few southern interlopers emerge onto the racecourse workground.

The string pass in front of the Ayr racecourse grandstand on an uncharacteristically bright morning.

affection for and affinity with her horses. She is also extremely hard working, thinking nothing of making the 900 mile round trip to Epsom if she thinks a horse has a chance. "This year we went down with two horses. Petite D'Argent won and the other was placed. You have to get the travelling in perspective. We're less than a couple of hours from Middleham and once you're on the motorways, nowhere is too far".

OWNERS:

G. Perratt; J.M.M. Richard; W.G. McHarg; David Landa; Peter Orr; M.S.J. Clydesdale; Jim Craig; J.C. Murdoch; Mrs.J.B. Russell; J.C. Park; K. McClelland; J.S. Douglas; Tom Carruthers; Mrs Helen Beattie; P. Caplan; Mrs Angela Wilson; Daniel Coupar; R.J. Wilkinson; Alli Namazee; John Muir; Margaret Crossbie; Blinds Direct; Lightbody of Hamilton.

NOTABLE HORSES:

Night Raid; Mount Athos; Swinging Junior; Roman Warrior; Current Gold; Dougalli

PAST TRAINERS:

John McGuigan; G. Laurence; Harry Whiteman; Nigel Angus; Charlie Williams; John Wilson

PAST ASSISTANTS:

Nigel Angus; Charlie Williams; Linda Perratt

HORSE TO FOLLOW:

Persian Charmer

Breckenborough House, Thirsk.

Lynda Ramsden

British racing would be a deal duller without the husband and wife team of Lynda and Jack Ramsden. When it was announced last year that the pair were planning to give up training, the news might not have been on a par with the Aga Khan decamping across the Channel but for aficionados of the art of preparing horses for handicaps, it would have been a serious impoverishment of the fun of the sport.

One might expect a yard associated with shrewd handicap coups and with a reputation for general all round cleverness to be a latterday Druids' Lodge in its attitude to publicity of any kind but this could not be further from the truth. One of the first things that strikes one about Breckenborough House is the disarming frankness of the incumbents. A conversation with Jack Ramsden about betting is the antithesis of the evasive, coy ritual one normally expects to have to go through with stable connections. "Lynda is the trainer. I'm interested in the betting side of things". Unlike most racing 'insiders' who, when asked whether they have backed a particular horse, will mumble something euphemistic and non-commital, Jack is frank and straightforward about his betting and its rewards. "It's paid for everything for years".

For Lynda Ramsden, the other half of the team, horses have always been a fundamental part of life - "I was encouraged into the Pony Club from an early age by a horsey mother" - and it is

Lynda Ramsden sorts out the work pattern for the day.

The horses flash past an electronic timer after a set exercise routine. Times are central to the Ramsden method.

The set-up at Breckenborough House involved the wholesale conversion of an existing farm.

she that supervises the training of the horses, making sure they are properly fed, exercised and well looked after. Jack is a background presence, monitoring times, blood, breeding, form and anything else that helps to narrow down the imponderables in the inexact science of betting. "Healthy horses, precisely monitored" as Jack puts it with characteristic economy.

As little as possible is left to chance. The training establishment at Breckenborough House, a few miles from Thirsk racecourse, was built from scratch to include all modern utilities: a swimming pool; laboratory; weighing machine; solarium and an automatically watered all weather gallop, complete with timing machine. In common with one of the couple's training heroes, Martin Pipe, what they do not have is grass gallops: "Everyone expects, when they go to Martin Pipe, to see acres of grass gallops, but all he has is an immaculately maintained 6 furlong all weather strip".

The all weather gallop at Breckenborough House is similarly well looked after, with a private bore hole feeding twelve pop-up sprayers per furlong. According to Lynda "without watering, you can get dangerous craters, but when it's wet and rolled, it's a different surface altogether. It binds together and provides quite a lot of spring". The one and a half mile long 'all weather' is arranged in a figure 9, the last two furlongs of which can be electronically timed, a central feature of the Ramsden method.

Timing serves a dual purpose: the assessment of ability and to assist in the monitoring of a steady aerobic work-rate. After a steady build up around the oval section of the track, the horses come down the chute of the figure 9, take a pull coming through the final turn, flash through a beam and, if they are being tested, work flat out for the last two furlongs, the last 100 yards of which is quite a stiff climb.

As the horses flash by, a figure registers on a small meter by the side of the track. Under 22 seconds is a quick time and nothing has yet broken the 20 second barrier. "A sprinter should be able to do 21 seconds" says Linda "and when a horse like Travelling Light does under 23 seconds, you know that he has the potential for a good turn of foot as well as stamina".

Such scientific exactitude throws the conventional vagueness of much gallops observation into question but Lynda Ramsden is unwilling to criticise others. "I think timing is a useful tool in the assessment of a horse. Jack loves interpreting and building up a pattern and timing is another way to do that. From a training point of view, I like to be able to know when they're really exerting themselves, to know when they're really finishing and when they're entitled to be falling in a heap".

Even the ostensibly recreational and therapeutic swimming of the horses can be used to check for deviations from an established pattern. "You can tell a lot from swimming. They're very individualistic in their swimming styles and you learn to recognise when they're holding themselves differently for some reason that may need attending to".

Jack describes himself as "an impatient man who is patient with horses". In stark contrast to many so-called gambling stables where horses are treated as mere gambling fodder, of no interest once the touch has been landed, Breckenborough House is replete with fully exposed older horses living long and happy lives. Horses like Cool Enough, a gallant old stager who is nursed through his various ailments to win "a race or two every year". "I'll keep anything that's capable of winning a race and that tries" says Jack. This indulgent attitude does not extend to "prattling owners with endless advice about what to do with useless home-bred fillies".

The well-named Crab 'n' Lobster is put through his paces.

Those that do show sufficient ability and application "not to be a waste of their owner's money" follow an unusually varied and stimulating routine at Breckenborough House, laid out by Lynda, who, despite being by her own admission 'conventionally horsey' is by no means hidebound by tradition when it comes to the diurnal patterns of training. "It seems strange to me, to keep equine athletes cooped up in dark boxes for 23 hours a day". "If they're stuffy, I'll ride them in the afternoon, turn them out in a paddock or have them on the horsewalker. Nothing stands in on a Sunday".

Safety in Numbers: a model of consistency.

The equine accommodation is purpose-built to meet very specific requirements. "I like the boxes to be big, light and airy with a view of what is going on elsewhere". Some of the most pleasant boxes in the yard were converted from Dutch barns and have immensely high ceilings. Draughts are mediated by Yorkshire boarding, which retains some warmth but which allows the circulation of air. The oppressiveness that can occasionally be felt in some stabling is completely absent and the sense of well-being that emanates from the equine inhabitants is palpable. Despite an injured shoulder, Cool Enough stands obediently to be photographed and Travelling Light sticks his neck out and grins with luxuriant pleasure as he is tickled by his trainer, who walks about her equine family with no fear of being kicked.

The superbly well-equipped Breckenborough House is about as far from one's old-fashioned preconceptions about a so-called gambling stable as it is possible to be. There is little doubt that Jack Ramsden is one of the cleverest and most consistently successful of Britain's professional punters but it is manifestly not a success achieved at the expense of the stable's inmates.

PAST TRAINERS:

None

NOTABLE HORSES:

Travelling Light; Daros;
High Premium

OWNERS:

Marquis of Downshire; David Thompson; Nicholas De Savary;
Colin Webster; Christopher Heath; K.E. Wheldon;
Helena Springfield Ltd; Flockton Developments; George Ridley;
Sillars Civil Engineering; A.J. Struthers; R.C. Moody; E.D. Kessly;
Mrs A.E. Sigsworth; David Faulkner; M. Charlton;
D.R. Price; C.J. Harper; M. Wong; B.D. Southam;
Mrs.J.D. Trotter; Yorkshire Decorators

Groundhill Farm, Lingdale.

Mary Reveley

The people of the mining village of Lingdale in Cleveland must be getting used by now to being asked directions to Groundhill Farm. "Oh, you mean the Reveleys. You go down past the Working Mens' Club and there's a little snicket on the right, just past the bungalows". The 'snicket' turns out to be an unsignposted track that appears to be leading to garages at the back of some semi-detached houses. From this unlikely entrance, the Reveley horsebox has emerged - driven, more often than not by Mary's husband, George - to plunder an ever-increasing number of racing prizes. It would be hard to imagine a more unassuming setting for what has become one of Britain's most successful dual-purpose yards.

Mary Reveley's family has farmed in the area for seventy years. "My father's father farmed at the top of the village and he got farms for most of his sons". Until recently, dairy cattle have been the main family concern: "the hardest work but the most profitable" according to Mary Reveley. Even now, with nigh on 100 horses competing for space on the farm throughout the year, a large herd of Friesians, overseen by younger son John, provides a useful extra string to the Reveley bow. It might seem overly cautious, given the yard's recent history, to be thinking

The Reveley success story has been achieved without the benefit of grass gallops.

The yard's residents taking a keen interest in events.

about fallbacks but prudence is a highly rated virtue at Groundhill Farm. Mary Reveley is under no illusions about the transitory nature of racing success. "There are any number of people you could name who were on top once and then fell away. When we increased the number of barns, we had them built so that they can always be used for something else".

The current army of horses has not appeared overnight. It was Mary's father that started the horsey ball rolling back in the 1950s. "My father always bred a few racehorses - he had the dam of a horse that won the Nunthorpe - and he had a few flat horses with Jack Calvert over at Hambleton". After graduating through the Pony Club and eventing scene, the young Mary Reveley developed a keen interest in point to pointing and racing, which she in turn passed on to her children, particularly Keith who is now assistant trainer.

It was "for the children" that Mary began training a few pointers back in the 1970s. With just three horses, the Reveleys notched up eleven wins, culminating in a controversial win in the Ladies' Hunter Chase final at Newcastle with a horse called Hello Louis. "He failed the dope test because our feed supplier hadn't cleaned some traces of Theobromine off their mixer". Even then, it would seem, there were people who resented the family's success. "The feed firm apologised and paid our prize money but for years people didn't stop whispering. It was a lot of fuss about nothing anyway: the dope hadn't done anything for his performance. He ran to within an ounce the next year. He even beat Prince Charles in a race".

Training the horses in those days was a rudimentary affair, consisting of long, hour and a half, hacks around the local hills. There were no special facilities for training and staff consisted of one stablegirl: "I've always been one for not doing things until I could afford them". Even now, with a hundred more horses, the Farm is not overstuffed with training aids and facilities. There is a stiff-looking six furlong all weather gallop that rises in two steep but steady inclines and a horse walker but not an awful lot besides. If there is a key to the Reveley family success, it does not lie in high-tech solutions.

Mrs Reveley is adamant that Lingdale is a more than adequate place to train (the results themselves are testimony enough). A brief spell at the famous Whitewall yard in Malton - "it might have been steeped in history but the boxes were dingy and narrow and all they looked out onto was the yard" - served to convince Mary and more particularly Keith, who was keen to try his hand elsewhere, that the grass is not always greener. "Apart from anything else, I like the privacy of this place. It is quite exposed here admittedly and in a bad winter it can get very cold but we seem to be getting mild winters these days and there's always the beach (at nearby Saltburn) if things get too bad".

A wry "that would be telling" is all Mary Reveley will divulge about her training methods in this secluded place, but admits that she does not work her horses too hard, never testing them against each other. Even with such a large string, Mary is still very much a hands-on trainer. "I think it's important to have an understanding of horses as individuals, not treating them all alike. I know every horse and know what feed they want and what their likes and dislikes are. It's also essential to get a good staff that like horses and aren't rough with them. Horses have to be happy to perform well".

American-style barns 'that can always be used for something else' house most of the yard's 100 plus inmates.

Stable star, Melottie, the apple of his trainer's eye. His dam provided Mary with her first ever success.

This contentment is palpable around the yard, which has an intimacy that belies the large number of horses. The pretty garden in front of the main house, replete with flowers and childrens' toys in equal measure, is bordered by two ranges of loose boxes. Mary's grandchildren play under the noses of long serving favourites such as Cab on Target, Melottie and Mr Woodcock, who seem to enjoy being in the thick of the action, observing everything that goes on. Melottie is a particular favourite, not just for the £140,000 that this admirably tough and consistent gelding has won over the years but because his dam, Lottie Lehmann, provided Mary with her first ever win against the professionals (the covering fee, incidentally, for Lottie's visit to sire Meldrum, was the princely sum of £250).

PAST TRAINERS:
None

NOTABLE HORSES:
Melottie; Cab on Target; Mr Woodcock; Dalkey Sound; Firm Price.

OWNERS:
P.D. Savill; R. Burridge; Lady Susan Watson; Geoff Pickering; Mrs Richard Stanley; D. Green; Mr and Mrs J.Williams; W.G Barker; J. McGovern; P.A.Tylor; Robbie Cameron; Peter Colquhoun; Mrs Lynne Firth; D. Playforth; G.G. Stevenson; C.C. Buckley; Ray Craggs; Malcolm Bailey; Mr Whybrow; R.Meredith; G. Nunn; H. Young; Mrs D. Horner; J. Good; A. Flanningan; Linda Leech; A. Harland; G.S. Brown; C. Anderson; Ronald Tindall; S.St.P. Burridge; W.H.Strawson; G.A. Fardon; A. Gauld; R. Malcolm Douglas; Mrs Susan Macdonald; Mrs Spensley; Mrs S. Whent; G. Fawcett; James Murray (Ballymena); R.H.M. Hargreave; A.J. Hilton.

HORSE TO FOLLOW:
Wellwotdouthink

Greystoke, Cumbria.

Gordon W. Richards

Three huge H's etched into the pink sandstone walls of Greystoke Castle stables proclaim that they once housed 'Henry Howard's Hunters'. Every season, when the Greystoke foxes had been hunted to Howard's satisfaction, that eccentric scion of the great Catholic family would hunt his pack of hounds from the Lake District to Gloucestershire and back across the parks and estates of England.

The same stables now house a mere half of the magnificent string of jumpers trained by the leading Northern National Hunt trainer, Gordon W. Richards, handler of such memorable horses as Little Bay, Lucius, Titus Oates, Hallo Dandy and latterly Carrick Hill Lad and Twin Oaks. Richards is married to Henry Howard's great grandaughter Joanie and smiles at the idea of his leisured predecessor. "What a comedown, all those grand people and now it's just me grafting away". At over sixty years of age, the lifestyle of Gordon W. Richards (the 'W' incidentally - standing for Waugh - was inserted during his apprenticeship by his old guv'nor, J.C. Waugh, to avoid confusion with the great Sir Gordon) is anything but leisured.

Despite the broken back which ended his riding career, Richards still rides out every morning, three lots if possible, and clearly enjoys the close contact with the animals, which are his pride and joy. 'Work' at Greystoke, however, is about as far removed as could possibly be imagined

Stable jockey Neale Doughty leads the string round the main yard at Castle Stables.

Henry Howard's Horses.

from life at any of the major training centres. The combined acreage of Greystoke Castle's park and the grounds of Rectory Farm, where the other half of the Richards' string is located, is about 4,000 acres and there is barely a road to be seen anywhere.

It is the ideal setting for the long term development and training of the traditional National Hunt type of horse. At the time of writing, Richards had just completed what he describes as a clean-out. "We only have about 60-70 jumpers in at the moment. We sold a few off and bought a lot of nice two and three year olds, which are nice jumpers for the future". Unlike many modern National Hunt trainers, Richards will not be tempted to run them on the flat in an attempt to recoup his investment.

"I don't mind having a few flat horses around the place but if I went into it I would want to do it properly and have a few good ones. You can't just do it casually, you'd need a different, smaller type of lad and everything would have to be changed around". Some of the new generation of young National Hunt stores will be sold on but the majority will be looked after and reared on Greystoke's rich pasture. "I'll feed them well and bring them on slowly. It's better that way because you know exactly what mileage is on them".

Richards' training methods have been refined over twenty six seasons on the estate, much of which he has developed himself, adding a fifty box yard at Rectory Farm to the existing fifty

Stable jockey (nearest) and trainer (far side) on the stiff Greystoke gallops.

The long trudge home. The Greystoke Castle park and the grounds of Rectory Farm stretch over 4,000 acres.

boxes at the Castle stables. The present numbers are a far cry from the early days in the late 1960s. When the young G.W. first acquired the lease of the stables in 1967, taking over from Tommy Robson (trainer of Champion Hurdle winner, Magic Court) he brought a grand total of five horses with him from his first base in Northumberland. Fortunately, one of these was stable star, Playlord, that grand old chaser, who went on to win a Great Yorkshire and a

A typical morning in the Lake District.

Scottish National among many other top races and, according to his trainer, "would have won the Gold Cup had the ground not come up heavy, which he hated". Since those early days, during which time the Greystoke handler has won just about every top race in the calendar, including two Grand Nationals with Hallo Dandy and Lucius, the essentials of the Richards' method of training have changed little, most of the ground rules having been learned much earlier in the Somerset-born trainer's career, during his time with the great Ivor Anthony (the trainer of Brown Jack and Royal Mail) at Wroughton, near Swindon in Wiltshire.

A lot of time is spent at Greystoke on the early preparatory work, walking and trotting around the seemingly endless variety of hills and paths available to the string on the estate. "We lob them around a lot in the fields around here and the typical National Hunt horse enjoys it. It's such a pretty place". For cantering and fast work, the gallops at Greystoke must be among the best private National Hunt work grounds in the country. On a big hill, leading up to the schooling grounds, is a stiff, curving climb of approximately one mile, all weather and grass next to one another in the shadow of a wood. The all weather gallop - an immaculate, chain-harrowed woodchip - was installed a number of years ago at a cost even then of £60,000. It performs a different function than most all weathers in Britain. During the National Hunt season at Greystoke, the 'natural' ground very rarely gets too firm; it is used primarily when the ground gets "either very wet or very frosty".

Although the all weather is well used, G.W. is old enough to remember the great trainers of the past getting by quite adequately without them. "Ivor Anthony always seemed to be able to work a horse. He'd put down a bed of straw or just keep them walking for a bit. If a horse is fit, a few easy days won't do him any harm, in fact they seem to enjoy the time off".

PAST TRAINERS:
Tommy Robson; Jack Pearson

NOTABLE HORSES:
Magic Court; Harvest Gold; Playlord; Titus Oates; Hallo Dandy; Little Bay; Lucius; Carrick Hill Lad; Twin Oaks

OWNERS:
Fiona Lady Arran; Lord Cavendish; Mrs Stewart Catherwood; Edinburgh Woollen Mill Ltd; John.D. Hamilton; R.J. McAlpine; R. Ogden; E.R. Madden; Major I. Straker; Mrs.D.A.Whitaker; Geoff Adam; J.N.G. Moreton; Richard Hall; Joseph Gordon; R.Tyrer; A.M. Proos; Alistair Duff; R. Loughlin; Ann Starkie; A.G. Martin; W.J. Peacock; Stanley Little; P. Hinchliff; Juliet Reed; Mrs Lynn Campion; C.W .Jenkins; Peter Cox; B.M. McKinney.

HORSE TO FOLLOW:
Whispering Steel

Rhonehurst, Upper Lambourn.

Oliver Sherwood

The tiny hamlet of Upper Lambourn, which nestles in a sheltered niche at the foot of the Downs, houses the greatest concentration of National Hunt horses in the British Isles. Stabled inconspicuously within a few acres of each other are a goodly proportion of the leading contenders for honours in the winter game. Take racing away from Upper Lambourn and there would be nothing left.

Oliver Sherwood's Rhonehurst yard lies at the heart of Upper Lambourn, sandwiched, appropriately enough, between Hobbs' Lane, which leads up to the training grounds, and the newly created Fulke Walwyn Way. Unusually, given the tight confines of the village, there is a feeling of spaciousness about Rhonehurst, which has a large, 34 acre paddock and a private all weather canter to itself. There is nothing but a steep hill to separate the yard from the rolling downland beyond; for a trainer with a large string, it is a major blessing there are are no public roads between the stables and the gallops, only a quiet, leafy lane.

Oliver Sherwood and stable favourite Arctic Call.

The yard itself is full of character, an old well-established core that is at least 100 years old, complemented by some tastefully achieved modern additions undertaken by Oliver Sherwood's predecessor, Richard Head. Sherwood himself has greatly expanded the yard's capacity from 28 boxes to 64, but without affecting the overall ambience.

There have been racehorses of one kind or another at Rhonehurst, or Ronehurst as it was formerly known, for at least a hundred years. At the turn of the century, one of the area's leading trainers, John Hallick, had a large and successful string in the yard, until he outgrew it in 1907 and moved to what were then larger premises at Waltham House (now Doug Marks' yard, 'Lethornes'). Rhonehurst then receded into the background for a few years, playing host to the small jumping string of one J. Rhodes, who trained both publicly and privately from the yard for a number of years.

Rhonehurst entered the limelight once more in 1932, when Harry Cottrill, who was then training at Seven Barrows, persuaded his old friend, former National Hunt jockey, Reg Hobbs (father of Bruce Hobbs) to take up training and found him what he thought was the ideal yard from which to do it: Rhonehurst.

Hobbs had been in America for many years after the end of his riding career, and those contacts stood him in good stead when he embarked on a training career. Wealthy American patrons, such as the Ambrose Clarks and Marion Scott, ensured a good quality of horse in the yard, but it was not until 1938, with the exploits of an extraordinarily brave little horse called Battleship, that Rhonehurst really hit the headlines.

Despite being barely 15 hands high and an entire horse of blue blooded stock (he was by the legendary US sire, Man O' War) Battleship managed, somehow, to confound his doubters and win the Grand National. According to those who remember him, Battleship jumped surprisingly well for a horse of his size and had "the heart of a lion". Almost as remarkable as Battleship's efforts at Aintree, was the riding performance of his seventeen year old jockey, Bruce Hobbs, the youngest rider ever to win the National, who drove the tiny eleven year old out, to win by a head in one of the most exciting Grand National finishes of all time.

Although none of the horses trained at Rhonehurst since have quite managed to reproduce the drama of Battleship's National, the yard has been a force to be reckoned with in the jumping world ever since. Another former National Hunt jockey, Matt Feakes, continued the Hobbs tradition to some effect in the 1950s and 1960s and Oliver Sherwood, in more recent years, has brought the yard into line with its major competitors with a dynamic programme of expansion and development.

Gone are the days when bad-legged Lambourn horses would stand in stagnant water for days on end to improve their circulation. Rhonehurst today is a well-appointed equine hotel, with

The well-appointed Rhonehurst yard has been sending out jumpers for over a century.

Coming home along Hobbs' Lane, named after Rhonehurst's most famous son.

The most recent addition to Rhonehurst's stabling is very much in-keeping.

The yard's blacksmith, Fred Fox, at work.

its own swimming pool, loose school, all weather canters and on-site blacksmith. Although the daily routine of three lots and evening stables has ostensibly altered little since the last century, in reality, National Hunt training patterns have undergone some significant changes. Following the Martin Pipe revolution, it is interval training, rather than long distance work, that is the order of the day in the Lambourn Bowl and horses with sore shins can be kept in work by exercising them in the pool. Oliver Sherwood maintains that, despite the cost, installing the pool at Rhonehurst is "the best thing I've done. Both Rebel Song and The West Awake, who won the Sun Alliance Hurdle and Chase respectively, would probably not have got to Cheltenham without the pool".

Despite keeping up with the times, Sherwood is still very much a product of the Fred Winter academy in his management of the yard and, more importantly perhaps, in his buying policy. "I know it sounds a bit corny, but you could do a lot worse than be a Fred Winter Mark II. Although we've got more horses here now than in the past, I don't believe in playing

When the leaves fall in Lambourn, it's a sure sign that the real work of the year is set to begin.

the numbers game. I'd rather have 40-50 good quality horses and take time with them than scratch around for second rate winners".

PAST TRAINERS:
J.F. Hallick; J. Rhodes; Reg Hobbs; M.W .Feakes; Bill Roach; Richard Head

PAST ASSISTANTS:
Nigel Twiston-Davies

OWNERS:
Christopher Heath; M.L. Oberstein; Lady Helen Smith; A. Boyd-Rochfort; Paul Stamp; P.A. Idris; Dr Ian Shenkin; P. Robeson; R. Waters; B.T. Stewart-Brown; R.B. Holt; Rory Larkin; Miss S.J. Cutliffe; Mary Arkle; Basil Samuel; I.A. Low; Denis Andrews; J.M.F. Dibben; J.C. South; John Stone; J. Dougall; H.M.Heyman; R.J. Clark; M.J. Marchant; David Bowkett; John Bolsover; Mrs F. Harvey; R.D.A. Kelly; M. Berger; M. Dorey; Mrs M.J. Heath.

NOTABLE HORSES:
Battleship; Medoc; Border Incident; Uncle Bing; Rebel Song; The West Awake; Cruising Altitude; Young Snugfit.

HORSE TO FOLLOW:
Celtic Town

Index

Horses, owners and trainers mentioned in the panels at the end of each chapter not included